EBENEZER

Record Book
1754–1781

Births, Baptisms, Marriages and Burials
of Jerusalem Evangelical Lutheran Church
of Effingham, Georgia,
More Commonly Known as Ebenezer Church

Translated and Edited by

George F. Jones

&

Sheryl Exley

CLEARFIELD

Published by Genealogical Publishing Co., Inc.
Baltimore, Maryland
1991

Library of Congress Catalog Card Number 90-84248

Reprinted for Clearfield Company by
Genealogical Publishing Company
Baltimore, Maryland
2015

ISBN 978-0-8063-2019-9

Ebenezer Church (from original photograph in the Hargrett Rare Book and Manuscript Library, University of Georgia Libraries)

Ebenezer Record Book
1754-1781

Contents

INTRODUCTION

These records report the births, baptisms, marriages, and deaths in the congregation of Jerusalem Church at Ebenezer, a church founded by religious exiles from Salzburg who settled in Georgia in 1734. These exiles had been brought to Georgia through the combined efforts of the Georgia Trustees and the Society for Promoting Christian knowledge, a missionary society based in London. For the exiles' religious care, the Society sought aid from the Francke Foundation, a charitable establishment in Halle in northeastern Germany, which supplied the Georgia Salzburgers with a series of capable ministers, the first two of whom were Johann Martin Boltzius and Israel Christian Gronau.

It was the duty of the Ebenezer ministers to report regularly to the Society all births, baptisms, marriages, and deaths in their congregation; and this they did faithfully. Unfortunately, all these reports are lost, let us hope only lost sight of, so the present edition is based on a church record book begun in 1754 and continued until 1800, which is now housed in the Library of Congress and catalogued as *Jerusalem Church Records*. Gronau having died before 1754, the entries were made by Boltzius and by Gronau's replacement, Hermann Heinrich Lemke, and later also by the additional ministers Christian Rabenhorst and Christoph Friedrich Triebner.

By 1754 many of the original Salzburgers had died and the survivors had been joined by Swiss and Palatines, but the largest addition was three large transports of Swabians from the territory of the Imperial City of Ulm on the Danube. These newcomers soon intermarried with the Salzburgers and so blended with them that all Lutherans of St. Matthew Parish were called Salzburgers.

These records were previously translated by the Reverend A. G. Voigt and edited and published at Savannah in 1929 by the Reverend C.A. Linn. Dr. Voigt must have been an excellent paleographer, for he solved some very difficult problems caused by the five different scripts, some of them quite crabbed. Even greater difficulty was caused by the fading of the ink on many pages, which was no doubt even worse in the photographic copies used by Dr. Voigt. Being unfamiliar with the names of Ebenezer's inhabitants, Dr. Voigt was dependent on the poor copy and therefore misread many names. As a result of these difficulties, Dr. Voigt created new families for Ebenezer, such as Asperger, Behrmann, Bitner, Denshardt, Eichelberger, Grein, Habor, Haut, Hebel, Heked, Kaehli, Kienegus, Kolcher, Keiter, Glauer, Koergter, Randfelder, Reidlinger, Reinshardt, Sauftleb, Scheinlaender, Schweinthofer, Schwinkhofer, Schwinthofer, Staub, and Tubly. The creation of these spurious names causes little harm, but the absence of the correct names does so. The name Burgermeister is interpreted as the noun "mayor" and the noun *Kirugus* (surgeon) is taken to be a name. There are also some errors in Christian names, such as Daniel for David and August for Ruprecht. Many of these errors were the fault of the German script itself. For example, it is hardly possible to distinguish between *Rh* and *Sch* in most calligraphies. When Baron von Reck returned to Europe via New England after bringing the first Salzburgers to Georgia, the printed version of his travelogue had him go from Connecticut to Massachusetts via Schrode Island.

More serious than these occasional misreadings was the practice of Anglicizing all Christian names even though the bearers themselves used only the German forms of their names. Henry Lewis and Ann Catherine would have been far less at home in Ebenezer than Heinrich Ludwig and Anna Catharina would have been. This practice can be blamed on the anti-German hysteria caused by British propaganda during World War I, when many German Americans renounced their ethnic origins. In this revision all Christian names have been restored to their original form for two reasons: to be more authentic and to make it easier to find these names in German church records and archives. For this latter purpose the German town of origin, when known, has been added in parentheses. Only a few of these appear in the Jerusalem records, while most have been found in the *Urlsperger Nachrichten*, the contemporary publication of the Ebenezer pastor's reports, or in other German sources. The nature and proper use of these records are clarified in the explanation introducing the appended genealogical index.

We wish at this time to thank Carol Warrington and Jan Plane of the University of Maryland Computer Science Center for their expert and patient aid in the difficult task of sorting and identifying the subjects in these records. We also wish to thank the R. J. Taylor, Jr., Foundation of Atlanta for generously covering the travel, typing, and other expenditures required for this research.

George Fenwick Jones   Sheryl Exley

Births and Baptisms, July 1756 – November 1781

1756

Johann Georg, son of Johann Georg Bunz and Barbara his wife, was born in the night between July 19 and 20 in Bethany, and was baptized on the 20th. The sponsors were Christian Biddenbach and Maria Michler.

Friedericka Margaretha, daughter of Johann Georg Bollinger and Barbara his wife, was born in Bethany, July 31, 1756, and baptized the same day. Sponsors were Valentin Deppe and his wife Margaretha.

Johannes, the son of Johannes Rentz and his wife Barbara, was born Aug. 15, 1756 at Ebenezer and baptized the same day. Sponsors were Christoph Kraemer, Ruprecht Zimmerebner, and Mrs. Catharine Lemcke.

Johanna Friedericke, the daughter of Friederich Helfenstein and his wife Blandina Magdalena, was born Aug. 28, 1756 in Abercorn, and was baptized Sept. 2 the same year. Sponsors were Johann Staehli, Sen. and his wife.

Jonathan Gottlieb, the son of Johann Ulrich Fezer and Barbara his wife, was born Aug. 30, 1756 in Ebenezer, and baptized there the same day. Sponsors were Ulrich Neidlinger and his wife and Simon Reuter.

Anna Margaretha, the daughter of Paul Fincke and his wife, was born Sept. 11, 1756, and baptized on the 12th. Sponsors were Ludwig Weidmann and his wife.

John Devis (Davis) had his daughter baptized on Sept. 23. [This entry stricken out, see next page.]

William, the son of McDanell and an unmarried German woman, was born at Hallifax, March 14, 1756, and was baptized here in Ebenezer Sept. 26 the same year. Sponsors were Matthias Zettler and Mrs. Cath. Bornemann.

Maria, the daughter of Joseph Schubdrein and Maria his wife, was born Oct. 2, 1756 in Ebenezer and baptized on the 3rd. Sponsors were Thomas Geschwandel and Sybilla his wife.

Catharina, the daughter of Joachim Hartstein and his wife Hanna, was born in Purrysburg, Oct. 12, and was baptized on the 18th, 1756 in Ebenezer. Sponsors were Johann Georg Mengersdorff and his wife and Catherina Rheinauer.

Samuel Leberecht, the son of Christian Riedelsperger and his wife Mary, was born Oct. 20, 1756 and baptized on the 22nd in Zion Church. Sponsors were Mr. Johann Martin Bolzius and his wife Gertraut.

Andreas, the son of Georg Fischer and his wife, was born Oct. 27, 1756 in Bethany and baptized the following day. Sponsors were Johann Caspar Wertsch and Mrs. Weinkauf.

Maria, the daughter of Heinrich Meyer and his wife, was born at Great Ogeechee, Jan. 3, 1753, and was baptized Oct. 19, 1756 in Jerusalem Church. Sponsors are Martin Daescher and his wife and Ursula Paulitsch.

Johann Heinrich and Daniel, twin children of the parents just named, were likewise born at Ogeechee, Oct. 3, 1755, and baptized Oct. 19th. Sponsors were Thomas Schweighofer and Martin Daescher and his wife.

Susanna, the daughter of James Waston and Elizabeth his wife, was born Jan. 23, 1756, and baptized Oct. 17th. The father acted as sponsor.

Sarah, an English child, daughter of John Davis and his wife Mary from the Ogeechee River, was born in Oct. 1756 and baptized in Jerusalem Church in Ebenezer on Sept. 23, 1756.

Georg Jacob, the son of Jacob Kuebler and Catherina his wife, was born in Goshen, Nov. 14, and was baptized on the 17th, 1756. Sponsors were Georg Scherraus and his wife; Jacob Kusmaul and his wife.

N. B. — Dec. 16, 1756 the baptized were reported to Mr. Broughton.

Unity, the daughter of John McCollom and Susannah his wife, was born Nov. 5, 1756 at Mount Pleasant and was baptized Dec. 13 the same year at Ebenezer. The father and mother together with Michael Connor acted as sponsors.

Maria, a Negro girl, was born on Theobald Keefer's [Kieffer's] plantation, Dec. 14, and baptized in his house the following day.

Dorothea, the daughter of Martin Lackner, Jun., and his wife Catherina Barbara, was born Dec. 19, 1756, and baptized on the 20th. Sponsors were Mr. Johann Martin Bolzius and his wife and Margaretha Kalcher.

Christian, the son of Mr. Johann Ludwig Meyer and his wife Barbara, was born Dec. 21, 1756, in the evening on his plantation and baptized on the 22nd. Sponsors were Mr. Johann Martin Bolzius, Mr. Hermann Heinrich Lemcke and Anna Barbara Rabenhorst.

1757

Johann Jacob, the son of Jacob Ihle and his wife Eva, was born in the night between Jan. 16 and 17, 1757, and baptized on the 20th. Sponsors were Jonas Mick and his wife; Johannes Staeheli, Jun., and his wife.

Abraham, the son of Leonhard Rheinauer and his wife Anna Barbara, was born Nov. 28, 1756, and baptized here Jan. 15, 1757. Sponsors were Friedrich Rieser and his wife and Nicolaus Winkler.

Christian Jonathan, the son of Christian Zipperer and his wife, was born Jan. 30, 1757 in Goshen and baptized Feb. 22nd. Sponsors were Veit Lechner and his wife.

Christiana Elizabeth, the daughter of Adam Treutle and
Margaretha his wife, was born early before day in Goshen, Feb.
13, 1757, and baptized at the same place on the 14th. Sponsors
were Paul Zittrauer and Apol. Rieser.

Johann Christoph, child of Johannes Gugel and his wife
Anna Maria, was born March 5, 1757, and baptized on the 6th.
Sponsors were Johann Christoph Kraemer and his wife; Ruprecht
Zimmerebner and his wife.

Christiana, child of Daniel Schubdrein and his wife Magdalena, was born March 8, 1757, and baptized on the 9th. Sponsors
were Johann Christoph Kraemer and his wife; Paul Mueller.

Sophia, child of Paul Francke and his wife Barbara, was born
March 17,1757, and baptized on the 18th. Sponsors were
Nicolaus Kronenberger and his wife and Ottilie, wife of Koennedy
[Kennedy].

Christian, child of Christian Oechsle and his wife Angelica,
was born in Bethany, March 27, 1757, and baptized the following
day. Sponsors were J. M. Paulitsch and Maria Muehler. Mrs.
Hapacher was also present.

Johannes, a Negro child, son of the Negro John and his wife
Sarah, was born in the night of April 5 to 6, 1757, and baptized
on the 6th on the Bevery plantation. Pastor Boltzius and his wife
were sponsors.

Margaretha, child of Caspar Heck and his wife, was born
April 7, 1757 at Bethany and baptized on the 8th. Sponsors were
Zimmerebner, Mrs. Kogler, and Mrs. Kalcher.

Tobias, child of Johann Ludwig Weidmann and his wife, was
born April 15, 1757, in the night, and baptized on the 17th.
Sponsors were Paul Fincke and his wife, Daniel Schubdrein.

Hanna Elisabeth, child of Johann Georg Ziegler and Anna
Catharina his wife, was born April 17, 1757, in the afternoon at

Ebenezer and baptized the following day. Sponsors were Johann Georg Haid, Anna Maria Flerl, and Barbara Kogler.

Maria Magdalena, child of Samuel Graeve and Anna Catharina his wife, was born May 2, 1759, and baptized on the 3rd. Sponsors were Mrs. Gertraud Boltzius, Mrs. Ott, and Johann Caspar Wertsch.

Maria Magdalena, child of Johann Georg Bechtle and his wife Eva Barbara, was born on the night of May 3, 1757, and baptized on the 4th. Sponsors were Christoph Kraemer and his wife and Margaretha Kalcher.

Israel, child of Theobald Kiefer and his wife Maria, was born July 30, 1757, on his plantation and baptized on the 31st. Sponsors were Christian Rabenhorst, Johann Flerl and wife, and Gertraud Boltzius.

William, son of Hugh Kenedy [Kennedy] and his wife, was born Aug. 12, 1757, at Mount Pleasant and baptized Aug. 17 in the church at Bethany. Sponsors were Paul Fincke and his wife.

N. B. — Johann Georg Schneider's wife gave birth to a stillborn son, Aug. 20, 1757.

Maria Elisabeth, child of Veit Lechner and his wife, was born in the night of Aug. 21, 1757, and baptized on the 22nd. Sponsors were Mrs. Catharine Lemcke, Christian Riedelsperger, and his wife.

Maria, daughter of Friedrich Kiefer and his wife, was born in the night of Aug. 23 to 24 and baptized on the 24th. Sponsors were Matthias Zettler and his wife and Maria Kalcher.

Hannah, daughter of Georg Kiefer and his wife, was born early on Aug. 22nd, 1757, and baptized the same day. Sponsors were Zimmerebener and Mrs. Zittrauer.

Johann Jacob, child of Jacob Tussing and his wife, was born Sept. 17, 1757, and baptized on the 19th. Sponsors were Paul Fincke, and Georg Faul and his wife.

The wife of Jacob Moses gave birth on Sept. 18th to a son, who died a few hours after birth but received lay baptism beforehand.

Christian, child of Matthaeus Biddenbach and his wife, was born in the night between Sept. 21 and 22, 1757, and baptized on the 23rd. Sponsors were Christian Biddenbach, Johann Michel, and Ursula Hangleiter.

Sulamith, daughter of Johann Martin Paulitsch, was born Oct. 3, 1757, and baptized the same day. Sponsors were Mrs. Gertraud Boltzius, Martin Lackner's wife, and Christoph Rothenberger.

Dorothea, child of Johann Peter Arnsdorf and his wife, was born Oct. 8, 1757, and baptized the same day. Sponsors were Georg Faul and his wife and the wife of Johann Rentz.

Peter, a Negro child, was born on the Good Harmony plantation, Oct. 14, 1757, and was baptized there on the 18th. Sponsors were Mr. Lemcke and his wife.

Jacob Israel, child of Christian Buerck and his wife, was born Oct. 23, 1757, and baptized the same day. Sponsors were Pastor Boltzius and his wife and Ruprecht Zimmerebener.

Robert, child of Robert Humfries and a woman named Charity, was born at Tuckasaking, June 1, 1757, and baptized Nov. 15 according to the English liturgy. The parents acted as sponsors.

Louise, daughter of Mr. Borneman and his wife, was born Sept. 21, 1757 in Halifax on the New Goettingen plantation and baptized by her grandfather, Johann Heinrich Greve.

Anna Maria, child of Georg Mueller and his wife Rosina, was born Dec. 4, 1757 in the night and baptized the same day. Sponsors were Conrad Eckhardt, Gnann, the wife of Haefner, and Paul Fincke's wife.

Gotthilf, child of Johann Michael Bohrmann and Eva Maria his wife, was born Dec. 12, 1757, in Goshen and baptized on the 15th. Sponsors were Johann Georg Dressler, and Matthaeus Wuest and his wife.

Johann Christoph, child of Nicolaus Kronberger and his wife, Elizabeth Margareth, was born Dec. 15, 1757, at noon and baptized on the 16th. Sponsors were Christian Birck, and Christoph Rottenberger and his wife.

Gratiosa, child of Paul Zittrauer and his wife, was born Dec. 12, 1757, and baptized the same day. Sponsors were Georg Kogler and his wife and Mrs. Gertraud Boltzius.

Johann, child of Georg Glaner and his wife Sibylla, was born Dec. 17, 1757, and baptized on the 18th. Sponsors were Johann Flerl and his wife.

Nathaniel, child of Carl Siegmund Ott and his wife Magdalene, was born on the morning of Dec. 20 and baptized in the afternoon of the same day. Sponsors were Christian Riedelsberger, Matthias Brandner, and Maria Flerl.

Hanna, child of Daniel Remshardt and his wife, was born Dec. 26, 1757, and baptized the same day. Sponsors were Simon Reuter, his wife, and Mrs. Kogler.

Josua, child of Martin Daescher and his wife, was born Dec. 30, 1757, and baptized the same day. Sponsors were Mr. Johann Martin Boltzius, his wife, and Christoph Rotenberger.

N. B. — Up to this point those baptized, deceased, and married to the end of the year 1757 have been reported to England.

1758

Maria Magdalena, daughter of Johann Hangleiter and his wife Ursula, was born Jan. 3, 1758, and baptized the same day. Sponsors were Johann Caspar Wertsch, Maria Flerl (Carl Flerl's wife), and Ursula Landfelder.

Surgeon Mayer's Negress gave birth to a boy on Jan. 2, who was baptized on the 5th and named Onesimus.

Johann Christoph, child of Urban Buntz and his wife, was born Jan. 11, 1758 in Bethany and baptized on the 12th. Sponsors were Zimmerebener, Kraemer, and his wife.

Israel, child of Gabriel Maurer and his wife Maria, was born Jan. 25, 1758, and baptized the same day. Sponsors were Georg Faul and his wife Rebecca.

Johann, child of Sebastian Fetzer and his wife Ursula, was born Jan. 28, 1758, and baptized on the 30th. Sponsors were Johann Michael Hirsch and his wife Regina Barbara.

Johann Gotthilf, child of Balthasar Rieser and his wife, was born in the night of Jan. 29 to 30, 1758, and baptized on the 30th. Sponsors were Johann Caspar Wertsch and Mrs. Paul Finck.

James, child of James Cacrum and his wife, was baptized in the seventh quarter year after his birth, Feb. 3, 1758 at Beaver Dam. Sponsors were Johann Heinrich Graeve, Andreas Greiner, and the mother.

Anna, child of John Brunson and his wife Mary, was born Feb. 3, 1757, in Graves County and baptized Feb. 6, 1758, in Halifax. The parents were the sponsors.

Anne Ree and Sarah [left unfilled] were baptized Feb. 9, 1758, at Briar Creek in the presence of the mother and Captain Green and [left unfilled] Kesee.

John, son of Immanuel Manyoras and his wife Maria, was born Aug. 1, 1757, at Black Creek and baptized Feb. 10 on Hudson's plantation. The mother herself acted as sponsor.

Daniel, son of John Williams and his wife Margareth, was born in Old Ebenezer, Feb. 2, 1758, and baptized on the 11th. Martin Daescher, his wife, and Georg Faul were sponsors.

Christian, child of Johann Hapacher and Agnes his wife, was born Feb. 12, 1758, and baptized the same day. Sponsors were Christian Biddenbach and Margareth Weinkauf.

Maria Magdalena, child of Georg Michel Weber and his wife, was born Jan. 31, 1758 in Goshen, and baptized Feb. 1. Sponsors were Thomas Geschwandel and Maria Flerl.

Daniel, son of Valentin Deppe and his wife Margaretha, was born Feb. 17, 1758, and baptized on the 18th. Sponsors were Georg Faul and Christoph Kraemer and his wife.

Johannes, child of Johann Georg Heid and his wife Eleanora, was born Feb. 23, 1758, and baptized the same day. Sponsors were H. Flerl, his wife Anna Maria, and Johann Georg Ziegler.

Johann Adam, child of Johannes Paulus and his wife Maria Ursula, was born Feb. 26, 1758, and baptized on the 26th, Oculi Sunday. Sponsors were Matthaeus Biddenbach, Johann Georg Gnann, and Ursula Hangleiter.

Elisabeth, daughter of Friedrich Treutlein and his wife, was born Feb. 24, 1758, and baptized March 4, 1758 on his plantation on Black Creek. Sponsors were Matthaeus Wuest and his wife Magdalena, and Catherina Schade.

Mr. Boltzius' Negress Maria gave birth to a girl, March 21, 1758, who was baptized the same day and named Christine.

Friedrich Gottlieb, child of Georg Schweiger and his wife Eva Regina, was born April 2, 1758, and baptized the same day.

Sponsors were Ruprecht Zimmerebener and his wife, whose place however was filled by young Lackner's wife.

Alice Heaton, child of Robert Heaton and Elisabeth his wife, was born Jan. 18 or 19, 1739, and was baptized April 15, 1758 in Ebenezer. Witnesses were William Ducker and her father Robert Heaton.

Joseph, child of Joseph Schubdrein and his wife Maria, was born in the night before Cantate Sunday, April 23, and baptized the same day. Sponsors were Thomas Geschwandel, Nicolaus Schubdrein, and Anna Maria Zuercher.

Christian, son of Ulrich Fetzer and his wife Barbara, was born May 11, 1758, and baptized on the 12th. Sponsors were Simon Reuter and Ulrich Neidlinger and his wife.

Elisabeth, child of Johann Georg Gnant and his wife, was born May 27, 1758, at Bethany and baptized on the 28th. Sponsors were Johann Georg Bechtle, the wife of Rahn, and Mrs. Kronberger.

Sarah, child of Jacob Metzker and his wife Margaretha, was born June 4, 1758, and baptized on the 5th. Sponsors were Pastor Johann Martin Boltzius and his wife and Mrs. Lemcke.

Maria Barbara, child of Barthel Mackh and his wife, was born June 10, 1758, and baptized the same day. Sponsors were Paul Finck, his wife, and Christian Biddenbach's wife.

Christiana Elizabeth, child of Balthasar Bacher and his wife Gertraud, was born July 10, 1758 in Goshen and baptized on the 12th. Sponsors were Leonhard Krauss and his wife and Margareth Zittrauer.

Carolina Catharina, child of Ludwig Weitmann and his wife Anna Eva, was born July 25, 1758, and baptized the same day. Sponsors were Paul Fincke and his wife.

Jonathan, son of Matthias Seckinger and his wife Anna Catharina, was born in the night before Aug. 1 and baptized Aug. 1, 1758. Sponsors were Johann Georg Ziegler, Georg Glaner, and his wife Sibyl.

John Southerland was born at Mount Pleasant, Sept. 22, 1757, and baptized in Ebenezer on the public Day of Repentance, Aug. 17, 1758. The mother's name is Jane Southerland. The father is already dead.

Johann, the child of Jacob Ihle and Eva his wife, was born before day Aug. 16, 1758, and baptized the same day. Sponsors were Jonas Mickh and his wife, John Staheli, Jun., and his wife.

Jonathan, child of Adam Treutlen and his wife, was born Aug. 22, 1758, and baptized on the 23rd. Sponsors were Theobald Kiefer and his wife and Johannes Kornberger.

Obadjah, son of Conrad Rahn and his wife Barbara, was born Sept. 1, 1758, and baptized on the 2nd. Sponsors were Martin Paulitsch, Matthias Zettler, and his wife.

Samuel, the child of Johann Gugel and his wife, was born in the night between Sept. 2 and 3, 1758, and baptized on the 3rd. Sponsors were Zimmerebener, Kramer, and his wife.

Samuel, child of Johann Ulrich Neidlinger and Waldpurga, was born Sept. 19, 1758, and baptized on the 20th. Sponsors were Ruprecht Zimmerebener and the widow Margaretha Zittrauer.

Daniel, child of Johann Friedrich Helfenstein and his wife, was born Sept. 22, 1758, in Abercorn and baptized Oct. 2. Sponsors were Veit Lechner and his wife.

Anna Christina, daughter of Christian Daescher and his wife, was born Sept. 26, 1758, in Goshen and baptized Oct. 2. Sponsors were Johann Staeheli, Jun., and his wife, representing Martin Daescher and his wife, and Christian Rabenhorst.

Hanna Elisabeth, daughter of Michael Rieser, was born Oct. 9, 1758, before day and baptized on the following day. Mr. Johann Ludwig Meyer and his wife and Hanna Elisabeth Wertsch were sponsors.

Rebecca, daughter of Johann Georg Niess, was born in the night between Oct. 14 and 15, 1758, and baptized on the following 15th. Sponsors were Georg Faul, his wife Rebecca, and Eleonora Haid.

Gottlieb, son of Stephan Millen, was born Oct. 15, 1758, before day and baptized the same day. Sponsors were Georg Faul, Zimmerebener, and Mrs. Gertraud Boltzius.

Dorothea, daughter of Veit Lechner and his wife, was born Dec. 3, 1758, in the night and baptized on the 6th. Sponsors were Christian Riedelsperger and his wife.

Abiel, son of Thomas Schweighofer and Hanna, now his wife, was born in the night between Dec. 15 and 16, 1758, and baptized on the 16th. Sponsors were Ruprecht Zimmerebener and Maria Riedelsperger.

Gilbert, son of James Grant and his wife, was born Dec. 8, 1758, in Abercorn and baptized on the 20th. Witnesses were Johann Staeheli, Jun., and his wife.

Anna Magdalene, daughter of Johann Philip Paulitsch, Sen., and his wife, was born in the night between Dec. 16 and 17, 1758, and baptized on the 17th. Sponsors were Johann Georg Gnann and his wife, also Mrs. Hangleiter.

Christiana Elisabeth, daughter of Georg Michel Weber and his wife, Maria Magdalena, was born Dec. 25, 1758, and baptized on the 26th. Sponsors were Thomas Geschwandel, Maria Flerl, and Hanna Elisabeth Wertsch.

1759

Elisabeth, child of Christoph Rotenberger and his wife Elisabeth, was born Jan. 16, 1759, and baptized the same day. Sponsors were Hans Schmidt and his wife Juliana.

Christiana, child of Matthaeus Wuest and his wife, was born Jan. 26, 1759, in the morning and baptized on the 31st. Sponsors were Johann Michel Bormann and Maria Eva his wife and Friedrich Treutlen and his wife Margaret.

Anna, child of Georg Heck and his wife Maria, was born Jan. 13, 1759 in Abercorn and baptized the 31st. Witnesses were Johann Goebel and Anna Barbara his wife.

Johann Gottlieb, child of Johann Georg Schneider and his wife, was born Feb. 18, 1759, and baptized on the 19th. Sponsors were Georg Faul and Leonard Kraus and his wife.

Johann Georg, child of Peter Arnsdorf and his wife Barbara, was born Feb. 26, 1759, and baptized the same day. Johann Rentz and Georg Faul and his wife were sponsors.

Anne, a child of English parents, Thomas Baxly and Verybee, was born March 8, 1759, and baptized on the 12th. Johann Martin Rheinlaender and his wife Maria were witnesses.

Anna, child of Caspar Heck and Anna his wife, was born March 11, 1759, and baptized on the 12th. Sponsors were Zimmerebener, Kalcher, and Rosina Mueller.

Ester, daughter of Matthias Zettler and his wife, was born March 22, 1759, and baptized March 23. Sponsors were Johann Caspar Wertsch and his wife and Mrs. Kronenberger.

Maria, a Negro child, was born on the plantation Good Harmony in Josephs Town on March 13, 1759 and baptized there on the 27th. Pastor Lemcke and Mrs. Bohrmann (representing Mrs. Lemcke) were the sponsors.

Margaretha, child of Johann Ludwig Meyer and his wife Barbara, was born March 31, 1759, and baptized April 2. Sponsors were Pastor Lemcke, Mrs. Rabenhorst, and Margareth Barbara the wife of Mr. Ewen, potter in Savannah.

Margaretha, daughter of Jacob Caspar Waldhauer and his wife Agnesia, was born April 8, 1759 in Goshen and baptized on the 11th. Sponsors were Margareth Barbara, the wife of Mr. Ewen in Savannah, Apollonia Rieser, and Andreas Seckinger.

Anna Margaretha, daughter of Jacob Tussing and his wife, was born in Bethany, April 10, 1759, and baptized on the 12th. Sponsors were Georg Faul and his wife Rebecca and the wife of Paul Fincke.

Johann Gottlieb and Samuel, twin children of Nicolaus Schubdrein and his wife Anna Maria, were born April 11, 1759. The younger son, Johann Gottlieb, received lay baptism by the midwife in the presence of Mrs. Krause and Angelica Kohleis, which was confirmed afterwards at the baptism of the first son, Samuel, which took place on the 11th. Sponsors were Joseph Schubdrein and his wife and Leonhard Krause. Sponsors for the younger son, Johann Gottlieb, were Pastor Boltzius, his wife, and Mrs. Krause.

Emmanuel, son of Theobald Kiefer and his wife Maria, was born in the night between April 28 and 29, 1759, and baptized on the 29th. Sponsors were Mr. H. H. Lemcke, Johann Flerl, and Mrs. Gertraud Boltzius.

Christian, son of Johann Georg Buntz and Barbara his wife, was born April 30, 1759, and baptized the same day. Sponsors were Christian Biddenbach and Maria Michel.

Albrecht Ludwig, child of Conrad Eckhardt and his wife Anna Maria, was born May 3, 1759, and baptized on the 4th. Sponsors were Heinrich Ludwig Buntz and Johann Georg Buntz and Maria Michel.

Daniel, son of Georg Rieser and his wife Anna Dorothea, was born May 8, 1759, and baptized on the 10th. Sponsors were Ruprecht Zimmerebener and Anna Margaretha Zittrauer.

On March 21, 1759, a daughter of Athanasius Thomas and his wife Rebecca was baptized, who was born at St. Matthew's Bluff in South Carolina, Oct. 28, 1758, and was named Sarah. The parents acted as sponsors.

Andrew, a boy 11 years old, son of Andrew Clemons and his wife Rebecca, was born May 28, 1747, in Congrees, and baptized March 22, 1759. Sponsors were [left unfilled] Thomas, David Thomas, and the boy's mother.

Johannes, son of Christian Oechsle and his wife Angelica, was born in the night before June 1, and baptized June 1, 1759. Sponsors were Johann Schuele and Agnes Happacher.

Maria Catharina, child of Johann Georg Bechtl and his wife Eva Barbara, was born June 8, 1759, and baptized the same day. Sponsors were Adam Treutle and his wife and Jacob Meyer, and his wife.

Johannes, child of Johann Georg Deininger and his wife, was born July 12 and baptized the same day. Sponsors were Christoph Rotenberger and his wife and Conrad Rahn.

Hanna Elisabeth, daughter of Johann Martin Paulitsch, was born July 15, 1759, and was baptized the same day. Sponsors were Christoph Rotenberger, Mrs. Gertraud Boltzius, and the wife of Martin Lackner.

Anna Magdalena, child of Johann Eppinger and Anna Barbara his wife, was born July 15, 1759, and baptized on the 21st. Sponsors were Matthias Aspacher, Anna Blitz, and Anna Unselt.

Anna Maria, daughter of Johann Pflueger and Barbara his wife, was born Aug. 2 in the evening and baptized on the 3rd. Sponsors were Kornberger and his wife and Mrs. Ott.

Samuel, son of Johannes Schneider and his wife Catharine, was born Aug. 8, 1759, and baptized on the 9th. Sponsors were Zimmerebener, Krause, and Mrs. Riedlsperger.

Maria Barbara, daughter of Johann Michel and his wife Maria, was born and baptized Aug. 12, 1759. Sponsors were Heinrich Ludwig Buntz and his wife Barbara.

Friedericka Margaretha, daughter of Johann Georg Bollinger and Barbara his wife, was born in the night between Aug. 21 and 22, 1759, and baptized on the 22nd. Sponsors were Christianus Biddenbach and Margareth Gnant.

Hanna Margarethe, daughter of Johann Jacob Heuseler and his wife Anna Maria, was born Aug. 29, 1759, and baptized on the 30th. Sponsors were Johann Ulrich Neidlinger, Margareth Leimberger, and Anna Margaretha Zimmerebener.

Johann Adam, son of Johann Klein and his wife Christina, was born in the night before Aug. 29, 1759, and baptized on the 29th. Sponsors were Johann Adam Treutle, Joseph Leitner, and Anna Margarethe Finck.

Johannes, child of Georg Kogler and his wife Barbara, was born Sept. 5, 1759, and baptized the same day. Sponsors were Johann Kornberger, Thomas Geschwandel, and Margaretha Zittrauer.

Elisabeth, daughter of Samuel Greves and his wife Margareth, was born Sept. 13, 1759, and baptized on the 14th. Sponsors were Johann Caspar Wertsch, Paul Zittrauer, and Mrs. Gertraud Boltzius.

Jonathan, son of Jacob Ihle in Josephs Town and his wife Eva, was born Sept. 30, 1759, and baptized on Oct. 4th. Sponsors were Johann Adam Treutle, Johann Michael Bormann, and his wife.

Samuel, son of Christian Zipperer and Anna Maria his wife, was born Oct. 2, 1759, and baptized on the 3rd. Sponsors were Georg Schweiger, Apollonia Rieser, and Lachner with his wife.

Hanna Elizabeth, daughter of Johann Hangleiter and Ursula his wife, was born Oct. 5, 1759, and baptized on the 6th. Sponsors were Johann Caspar Wertsch, Hanna Elizabeth his wife, and Ursula Landfelder.

Jonathan, son of Gabriel Maurer and his wife, was born Oct. 6, 1759, and baptized on the 7th. Sponsors were the smith Georg Faul and his wife Rebecca.

Eleonora, child of John Cocklet and Catharina his wife, was born July 21, 1759 at Beaver Dam and baptized Oct. 20th. Sponsors were Johann Caspar Wertsch and John Wheatly.

Christian Israel, child of Johann Caspar Wertsch and Hanna Elisabeth his wife, was born Nov. 22, 1759, and baptized the following day. Sponsors were Johann Flerl and his wife.

Conrad, son of Johann Paul Francke and his wife Barbara, was born Nov. 22, 1759, and baptized on the 23rd. Sponsors were Hugh Cannady [Kennedy], Conrad Rahn, and Gugel's wife.

N. B. − Up to this point those baptized have been reported to London.

1760

Salome, daughter of Heinrich Meyer and his wife Maria, was born on the Ogeechy River in Georgia, Feb. 1, 1758, and baptized Jan. 3, 1760. Sponsors were Johann Adam Treudlen, his wife, and Ursula, wife of Martin Taescher.

Judith, child of the same parents, born June 21, 1759, and baptized on the just named Jan. 3, 1760. Martin Taescher and his wife and Mrs. Treutlen acted as sponsors.

Johann Georg, child of Johannes Schiehle and Anna his wife, was born early on Jan. 17, 1760, and baptized the same day. His sponsors are Johann Georg Deininger and his wife Barbara Deininger, also Caspar Heck and his wife.

Maria, a Negro child on the land of the Messrs. von Muench, was born in the night before Jan. 11, 1760, and baptized on the 18th. Pastor Boltzius and his wife were the sponsors.

Anna Catharina, daughter of Martin Taescher and Ursula his wife, was born Feb. 1, 1760, and baptized the following day. Sponsors were Johann Adam Treutlen and his wife and Mrs. Boltzius.

Catharina, daughter of Michael Rieser and Apollonia his wife, was born Feb. 1, 1760, and baptized on the following day. Sponsors were Surgeon Mayer and his wife and Mrs. Hanna Elisabeth Wertsch.

Daniel, child of Christian Birck and Ursula his wife, was born Feb. 24, 1760, and baptized on the 25th. Sponsors were Pastor Boltzius and his wife and Ruprecht Zimmerebener.

Salome, child of Thomas Baxly and Verybee his wife, was born [left unfilled], and baptized Feb. 24, 1760. She was at this time something over six years old. Sponsors were Johann Martin Rheinlaender and Maria his wife and Maria Magdalena Kalcher.

Benaja, child of Thomas Schweighofer and Hanna his wife, was born Feb. 27, 1760, and baptized on the 28th. Sponsors were Ruprecht Zimmerebener and Elisabeth Kogler.

Gottlieb, son of Johannes Rentz and his wife Barbara, was born March 20, 1760, and baptized the same day. Sponsors were Christoph Kraemer, Ruprecht Zimmerebener, and Mrs. Cath. Lemcke.

Elisabeth, child of Adam Treutle and Margaretha his wife, was born April 8, 1760, and baptized on the 9th. Sponsors were

Johann Kornberger and Lucia his wife and Mrs. Hanna Elizabeth Wertsch.

Maria Catharina, child of Johann Georg Schneider and Maria Barbara his wife, was born April 21, 1760, and baptized the same day. Sponsors were Leonhard Kraus, his wife Barbara, and Rebecca Faul.

The wife of Johann Philip Paulitsch gave birth to a stillborn girl, April 21, 1760.

Johannes, son of Jacob Gnann and his wife Maria Margaretha, was born in the night before April 23, 1760, and baptized the same day. Sponsors were Christoph Kraemer, G. Faul, and Rebecca his wife; M. Magd. Schubtrein.

John, 4 years old, born Jan. 24, 1756.

Mary, 3 years old, born March 24, 1757.

Sarah, 1 year old, born April 4, 1759.

These children of James Larrimor and Rebecca his wife, were baptized at the same time, April 26, 1760. The parents themselves were the sponsors.

Maria, the little daughter of Joseph Schubtrein and Maria his wife, was born April 26, 1760, and baptized on the same day. Sponsors were Nicolaus Schubtrein and Anna Maria his wife.

Georg, son of Georg Gruber and his wife Elisabeth, was born in the night after Ascension Day, March 15, 1760, and baptized the following 16th. Sponsors were Christian Biddenbach, Jacob Mohr, Sophia Biddenbach, and Ursula Landfelder.

Michael, child of Bartholomaeus Mackh and Maria his wife, was born May 20, 1760 early before day and baptized the same day. Sponsors were Michael Weinkauf, Paulus Finck, and Anna Margaretha his wife, and Sophia Biddenbach.

Lucia, daughter of Matthias Seckinger and his wife, Anna Catherina, was born June 7, 1760, and baptized on the following day, the first Sunday after Trinity, in Jerusalem Church. Sponsors were Johann Georg Ziegler and his wife and Sybilla Glaner.

Johann Georg, child of Johann Georg Niess and Catharina his wife, was born in the night before June 12, 1760, and baptized the same day. Sponsors were G. Faul and his wife Rebecca and Jacob Mohr, Sen., and his wife.

Lydia, child of Conrad Rahn and Anna Barbara his wife, was born before day June 15, 1760, and baptized the same day, the second Sunday after Trinity. Sponsors were Matth. Zettler and Elisabeth Catharina his wife, also Ursula Paulitsch.

Christian Philip was born July 8, 1760, before day, and baptized in the afternoon. He is the son of Johann Caspar Greiner and Carolina Magdalena his wife. Sponsors were Georg Faul and Mr. Rabenhorst and his wife.

Lydia, daughter of Jacob Caspar Waldhauer and his wife Agnesia, was born July 16, 1760, and baptized on the 17th. Sponsors were Andreas Seckinger, Apollonia Rieser, and the wife of Mr. Ewen in Savannah, who was represented by Mrs. Mayer.

Maria Judith, child of Johann Christoph Heintz and his wife Regina Barbara, was born July 17, 1760, and baptized the 18th. Sponsors were Pastor Lemcke and his wife, and the wife of Chr. Kraemer.

Jacob, son of Sebastian Haselauer and his wife Elisabeth, was born Aug. 20, 1760 before day, and baptized in the afternoon of the same day. Sponsors were Christian Oechsle, Johann Georg Buntz, and Anna Heck.

Johann Christoph, son of Sebastian Fetzer and his wife Ursula, was born in the night before Aug. 21, 1760, and baptized the 21st. Sponsors were Johann Christoph Heintz and Regina Barbara Heintz.

Christian, a Negro child, was born at the Mills in the night between Aug. 20 and 21, 1760, and baptized the same day. Mr. Flerl and Mrs. Wertsch were the sponsors.

Conrad, child of Johann Georg Deininger and Anna Barbara his wife, was born Aug. 30, 1760, at midday and baptized in the evening. Sponsors are Johannes Paulus, Conrad Rahn, and his wife.

Michael, son of Balthasar Rieser and his wife Maria, was born Sept. 6, 1760, in Bethany and baptized on the 7th, the 14th Sunday after Trinity. Sponsors were Michael Rieser, Master Wertsch, and Mrs. Gertraud Boltzius.

Catherina, child of Jacob Metzcher and his wife Margaretha, was born Sept. 10, 1760, and baptized on the 11th. Sponsors were Mr. Johann Martin Boltzius and his wife and Mrs. Catharina Lemcke.

Hanna Elisabeth, daughter of Johann Georg Ziegler and his wife Catharina, was born Sept. 20, 1760, and baptized on the following 16th Sunday after Trinity. Sponsors were Joh. Georg Haid, Mrs. H. Flerl, and Mrs. Kogler.

Hanna Elisabeth, daughter of Daniel Schubtrein and his wife Magd., was born Sept. 23, 1760, in the forenoon and baptized in the afternoon. Sponsors were Mr. Kraemer and his wife and Mrs. Weitmann.

Nathanael, son of Matth. Biedenbach and his wife, was born Nov. 6, 1760, before day and baptized the same day immediately after the Thanksgiving sermon. Sponsors were Joh. Hangleiter and his wife.

Samuel, son of Jacob Ihle and his wife, was born in the night before Nov. 7, 1760, and was baptized on the 8th. Sponsors were Johann Adam Treutlen and Michael Bohrmann and his wife.

N. B. — Up to this point those baptized have been reported to the Society.

Hanna, daughter of Gabriel Maurer and his wife Anna, was born Nov. 27, 1760, and baptized the 28th. Sponsors were Carl Ott and his wife Anna Magdalena.

Abigail, daughter of Johann Georg Gnann and his wife Anna, was born in Bethany in the night between Nov. 29 and 30, 1760, and baptized on the 30th. Sponsors were Conrad Rahn, Georg Bechtel, Mrs. Kronberger, and Mrs. Rahn.

Anna Barbara, child of Urban Buntz and his wife Margaretha, was born Dec. 3, 1760 in the forenoon and baptized in the afternoon. Sponsors were Christoph Kraemer and his wife, Ruprecht Zimmerebener, and the wife of Ludwig Buntz.

Aaron, a Negro child, was born Dec. 7, 1760, on Zettler's land and baptized on the 8th. Zettler and his wife were the sponsors.

1761

Johannes, child of Johannes Heinle and his wife Maria, was born Dec. 30, 1760, and baptized Jan. 1, 1761. Sponsors were Georg Faul and his wife Rebecca.

David, son of Johann Ulrich Neidlinger and his wife Waldpurga, was born Jan. 6, 1761, and baptized the same day. Sponsors were Rupr. Zimmerebener and Anna Marg. Zittrauer.

Christiana, daughter of Johann Jacob Haeuseler and his wife Anna Maria, was born March 19, 1761, and baptized on the same day. Sponsors were Joh. Ulrich Neidlinger, Mrs. Leimberger, and Anna Marg. Zimmerebener.

Johannes, child of Johannes Gugel and his wife Anna Maria, was born here April 1, 1761 in the evening and baptized on the 2nd. Sponsors were Joh. Christoph Kraemer and his wife and Ruprecht Zimmerebener.

Jonathan, son of Peter Arnsdorff and his wife Barbara, was born early on April 6, 1761, and baptized the same day. Sponsors were Christoph Kraemer, Johann Kornberger, and Ursula Landfelder.

Johann Paulus, son of Jacob Tussing and his wife Maria, was born April 16, 1761 in the evening, and baptized the 17th. Sponsors were Paul Fincke and his wife and Georg Faul and Rebecca his wife.

Johanna, daughter of Mr. Johann Ludwig Mayer and his wife Barbara, was born April 13, 1761, in the evening after 9 o'clock and baptized the 17th. Sponsors were Pastor Boltzius and Mrs. Catharina Lemcke and Margaretha Ewen in Savannah.

Margaretha, a child of English parents John Couchlan and Catharina his wife, was born Dec. 4, 1760, and baptized May 4, 1761. The place of sponsors was taken by the mother and Joh. Cas. Wertsch and Chr. Birck.

Gratiosa, daughter of Johann Martin Paulitsch and his wife Ursula, was born at midnight before May 7, 1761, and baptized the same day. Sponsors were Christoph Rottenberger, Mrs. Boltzius, and Mrs. H. Elis. Wertsch.

Martha, Master Kiefer's Negro girl, was born in the night between May 3 and 4, 1761, and baptized on the 12th. Master Kiefer and his wife acted as sponsors.

Rebecca, daughter of Johann Georg Schneider and his wife Barbara, was born June 1, 1761 early in the night and baptized on the 2nd. Sponsors were Georg Faul and Rebecca his wife and Mrs. Krause.

Nathanael, son of Matthias Zettler and his wife Elisabeth, was born June 7, 1761, and baptized the same day. Sponsors were Joh. Caspar Wertsch and his wife and Theobald Kiefer.

Maria, Matth. Aschbacher's Negro girl, was born in Savannah, Jan. 6, 1761, and baptized in Bethany, June 12, 1761. Sponsors were Aschbacher and his wife.

Thomas, son of Thomas Schweikhofer and Hanna his wife, was born July 8, 1761, and baptized the same day. Sponsors were Ruprecht Zimmerebener and Elisabeth Kogler.

Paulus, child of Barthol. Mackh and his wife, was born July 16, 1761, in Bethany and baptized the 17th. Sponsors were Paulus Finck and his wife, Michael Weinkauff, and Sophia Bidenbach.

Samuel, Zischler's son, appears to have been forgotten to be recorded. He was born May 12, 1761, and baptized the 13th. Pastor Boltzius and his wife were sponsors.

Johann Wilhelm, son of Johann Heinrich Busch and Scholastica his wife, was born in Savannah, July 4, 1761, and baptized on the 11th. Sponsors were Johann Adam Keller and Anna Maria Lang.

Carl, a Negro child on Mr. von Muench's land, was born in the forenoon and baptized in the afternoon of Aug. 18, 1761. Sponsors were Mr. Johann Carl von Muench and his wife, who were represented by Pastor Heinrich Lemcke and Mrs. Kraemer.

Anna Margaretha, daughter of Joh. Georg Pechle and his wife Barbara, was born Aug. 20, 1761, and baptized the same day. Sponsors were Jacob Mayer and wife and Mrs. Treutlen.

Angelica, daughter of Caspar Heeck and Anna his wife, was born in Bethany, Sept. 5 in the afternoon, and baptized on the 6th in Jerusalem Church. Sponsors were Zimmerebener, Mrs. Mueller in Bethany, and Mrs. Kalcher.

Jonathan, child of Johannes Schneider and Catharina his wife, was born Sept. 6, 1761, and baptized on the same day in Zion Church. Sponsors were Zimmerebener and Krause and his wife.

Johann Georg, child of Joh. Georg Buntz and his wife, was born Sept. 13, 1761, in Bethany and baptized the same day. Sponsors were Christian Bidenbach and Mrs. Michler.

Johann Andreas, child of Joh. Christoph Heintz and his wife Regina Barbara, was born Sept. 20, 1761, and baptized the same day. Sponsors were Mr. Heinrich Lemcke and his wife and Christoph Kraemer.

Mrs. Rabenhorst gave birth to a son on Sept. 18, 1761, which died at birth. God comfort the sorrowing parents for this bereavement with His heavenly comfort.

Christian Israel, child of Johann Georg Haid and Eleanora his wife, was born in the night between July 27 and 28, 1761, and baptized on the 28th in Zion Church. Sponsors were Hans Flerl and his wife and Joh. Georg Ziegler.

David, son of Johannes Klein and his wife Christina, was born in Bethany Oct. 13, 1761, in the afternoon and baptized on the 14th in Jerusalem Church. Sponsors were Joseph Leitner, Johann Gugel and Anna Barbara Rahn.

Johann Jacob, son of the tailor Georg Uland, was born in Acton Oct. 16, 1761, and baptized Oct. 21. Sponsors were Jacob Theuss and his wife Dorothea.

Johanna Christiana, child of Johannes Rentz and his wife Barbara, was born in the night between Nov. 22 and 23, 1761, and baptized on the 23rd. Sponsors were Mrs. Lemcke and Mrs. Faul.

Up to this point the baptized have been reported.

Benaja, son of Mr. Joh. Caspar Wertsch and his wife Hanna Elisabeth, was born Nov. 29, 1761, and baptized the 30th. Sponsors were Joh. Flerl and his wife and Rup. Zimmerebener.

Margaretha Dorothea, child of Georg Michael Weber and Maria Magdalena his wife, was born in the night before Dec. 29, 1761, and baptized on the 30th. Sponsors were Mr. Joh. Caspar Wertsch and Hanna Elisabeth his wife, both of whom were represented by Joh. Ulrich Neidlinger and the wife of John Staeli, Jun., and Maria Flerl.

1762

Samuel, son of Nic. Schubtrein and his wife Anna Maria, was born the night before Jan. 22, 1762, and baptized the same day. Sponsors were Joseph Schubtrein and Maria his wife and Krause.

Salomo, son of Joh. Georg Gnann and his wife Anna, was born on Sunday, Jan. 24, 1762, late in the evening and baptized Jan. 25th. Sponsors were Conrad Rahn and his wife and Joh. Georg Pechtle.

Johannes, son of Johann Pflueger and his wife Barbara, was born in the night before Jan. 27, 1762, and baptized on the 27th. Sponsors were Johann Kornberger and his wife Lucia and Johann Georg Heckel.

Salome, daughter of Paul Finck and his wife Margaretha, was born in the night between Jan. 31 and Feb. 1, 1762, and baptized Feb. 1. Sponsors were Ludwig Weitmann and his wife.

Benjamin, child of Martin Taescher and his wife Ursula, was born Feb. 8, 1762, and baptized on the same day. Sponsors were Pastor Boltzius and his wife and Mr. Adam Treutle.

Amalia, a Negro girl, was born in Savannah, July 1, 1761, and baptized Feb. 9, 1762 in Jerusalem Church. Sponsors were Pastor Lemcke and his wife.

Dorothea, daughter of Joh. Adam Treutlen and his wife Margaretha, was born Feb. 21, 1762, after midnight, and baptized on the afternoon of the same day. Sponsors were Master Kiefer and his wife and Master Wertsch.

Tobias, son of Georg Fischer and his wife Anna Dor., was born March 12, 1762, in the evening and baptized on the 14th. Sponsors were Zimmerebener, Mr. Wertsch, and the sister-in-law. This child is a twin; the other died immediately after birth.

Joh. Philip Paulitsch's wife gave birth to a stillborn daughter March 25, 1762.

Jonathan, son of Conrad Rahn and his wife Anna Barbara, was born in the night between March 26 and 27, 1762, and baptized the 27th. Sponsors were Zettler and wife and Joh. Martin Paulitsch.

Sebastian Fetzer's wife gave birth to a stillborn daughter April 2, 1762.

Lucia, daughter of Johann Jacob Metzcher and his wife Margaretha, was born April 15, 1762, in the evening and baptized on the 16th in Jerusalem Church. Sponsors: Johannes Kornberger and Mr. Kiefer and his wife.

Thomas, a Negro child on the land of Messrs. von Muench, was born May 5, 1762, and baptized on the 6th. Sponsors were Pastor Boltzius and his wife.

Johannes, son of Johann Hangleiter and his wife Ursula, was born May 12, 1762, early, and baptized on the same day. Sponsors were Mr. Wertsch and his wife.

Sulamith, a Negro girl, was born in Master Kiefer's family, May 6 and baptized the 17th, 1762.

Catharina, daughter of Joh. Georg Deininger and his wife Anna Barbara, was born June 30, 1762, before day and baptized in the afternoon. Sponsors were Johann Paulus and his wife and Mrs. Rahn.

Johann Conrad, child of Johann Conrad Frickinger and his wife Barbara, was born Dec. 17, 1761, in Fort Argyle, and baptized July 14, 1762, by Pastor Boltzius. Sponsors were Georg Winckler and his wife and Gottlieb Steheli and his wife.

Hanna, daughter of Christian Steiner and Dorothea his wife, was born Aug. 9, 1762, and baptized the same day. Sponsors were Ruprecht Zimmerebener and Anna Margaretha Zimmerebener.

Sarah, Matthias Aschbacher's Negro girl, was born Aug. 2, 1762, and baptized on the 9th. Sponsors were Matthias Aschbacher and his wife.

Maria, daughter of Michael Rieser and his wife Apollonia, was born Sept. 25, 1762, and baptized on the 26th. Sponsors were Mr. Mayer and his wife and Mrs. Wertsch.

Jonathan, son of Jacob Gnann and his wife Margaretha, was born Sept. 30, 1762, in the evening and baptized Oct. 1st. Sponsors were Zimmerebener and Faul and his wife.

Johann Jacob, son of Georg Gruber and his wife Elisabeth, was born Oct. 13, 1762, in Bethany and baptized the same day. Sponsors were Christian Biddenbach and wife, Johann Paulus and wife.

Johann, son of Johann Heinle and his wife Maria, was born Oct. 11, 1762, and baptized the following day. Sponsors were Faul and wife.

Salome, child of Johannes Gugel and Anna Maria his wife, was born Nov. 10, 1762, and baptized on the 11th. Sponsors were Zimmerebener and his daughter Anna Margaretha and Mrs. Kraemer.

N. B. — Up to this point those baptized reported, also the two Nos. 618 and 619.

Johannes, child of Johann Georg Schneider and his wife Barbara, was born Dec. 11, 1762, and baptized on the 12th. Sponsors were Faul and his wife.

Catharina Margaretha, daughter of Gabriel Maurer and his wife Anna, was born Dec. 14, 1762, and baptized the same day. Sponsors were Carl Siegmund Ott and his wife.

Timothaeus, child of Johann Georg Zittrauer and his wife Catharina, was born in the night between Dec. 6 and 7, 1762, and baptized in the forenoon of the 7th in Zion Church. Sponsors were Johann Casper Wertsch and his wife.

Christian, child of Daniel Schubtrein and his wife Magdalena, was born Dec. 11, 1762, in the morning and baptized shortly before evening. Sponsors were Paul Mueller and Weitmann and wife.

Christian, son of Johann Paul Francke and his wife Barbara, was born in Bethany, Dec. 11, in the afternoon, and was baptized on the 12th. Sponsors were Master Kiefer and Conrad Rahn and his wife.

Catharina and Hanna, two Negro girls, were born on Mr. Rabenhorst's land, Dec. 22, 1762. These twins were baptized also on the same day.

Salome, daughter of Thomas Schweighofer and Hanna his wife, was born in the night before Dec. 24, 1762, and baptized on the 24th. Sponsors were Ruprecht Zimmerebener, Elisabeth Kogler, and Judith Flerl.

1763

Maria, daughter of Johann Georg Ziegler and Catharina his wife, was born in the night between Jan. 2 and 3, 1763, and baptized in the afternoon of the 3rd in Zion Church. Sponsors were Johann Georg Haid, Mrs. A. M. Flerl, and Mrs. B. Kogler.

Johanna, daughter of an Englishman, namely the deceased Thomas Baxle and his wife Ferribay, six years old, was baptized Feb. 2, 1763, in Bethany. Sponsors were Maria and Matthias Weinkauff.

Anna Catharina, daughter of Matthaeus Biddenbach and his wife Anna Margaretha, was born in the night between Feb. 23

and 24, 1763, and baptized on the 24th. Sponsors were Hangleiter and wife.

David Schubtrein, son of Joseph Schubtrein and his wife Maria, was born March 18, 1763, before day and baptized on the same day. Sponsors were Nicolaus Schubtrein and his wife An.

Sarah, daughter of Heinrich Meyer and his wife, was born early March 21, and baptized the same day. Sponsors were J. A. Treutlen, his wife, and Mrs. Taescher.

Joseph, son of Jacob Tussing and his wife, was born April 22, 1763, and baptized on the 23rd. Sponsors were Paul Finck and his wife and Georg Faul.

Daniel, a Negro boy, was born May 13, 1763, and baptized on the 17th. Sponsors were Pastor Lemcke and his wife.

Elisabeth, daughter of Johann Georg Rieser and his wife Sibylla Regina, was born July 19, 1763, in the evening and baptized on the 20th. Sponsors were Faul and his wife, Jacob Mohr, Sen., and his wife.

Jonathan, child of Johann Martin Paulitsch and his wife Ursula, was born July 21, 1763, and was baptized in the afternoon of the same day. Sponsors were J. C. Wertsch, Rottenberger, and Mrs. Boltzius.

Rosina, daughter of Matthias Zettler and his wife Catharina Elisabeth, was born Aug. 9 in the evening and baptized the following afternoon. Sponsors were Mr. Kieffer and his wife and Mrs. Kronberger.

Maria and Thomas, twin children of Barth. Mackh and his wife Maria, were born Aug. 13, 1763, in the evening and baptized on the 14th. Sponsors for Maria were Paul Finck, his wife, and Sophia Bidenbach; for Thomas, Johann Peter Freyermuth, Thomas Mackh, and Maria Weinkauff.

Catharina, daughter of Mr. Johann Casper Wertsch and his wife Hanna Elisabeth, was born Aug. 13, 1763 in the evening and, because the child was feeble, it received lay baptism, which was confirmed on the 15th, when the sponsors were Mr. Joh. Flerl and wife.

Jonathan, child of Johann Klein and his wife Christina, was born Aug. 19, 1763, before evening and baptized on the 20th. Sponsors were Mr. Treutlen, Joseph Leitner, and Anna Barbara Deininger.

Timothaeus, son of Christian Birck and his wife Ursula, was born Sept. 17, 1763, and baptized on the 18th. Sponsors were Pastor Boltzius and his wife and Ruprecht Zimmerebener.

Christian, a Negro boy, was born in Schweiger's house, Sept. 28, 1763, and baptized the 29th. Sponsors were Georg Schweiger and his wife.

David, a Negro boy, was born on Mr. Rabenhorst's plantation, Sept. 29th, and baptized on the 30th. Sponsors were Mr. Rabenhorst and his wife.

Maria, daughter of Surgeon Mayer and his wife, was born Oct. 6, 1763, in the evening and baptized on the 11th. Sponsors were Pastor Boltzius, his wife, and Apollonia Rieser.

Matthaeus, son of Ludwig Weitmann and his wife Anna Eva, was born in the night between Nov. 8 and 9, 1763, and baptized in the afternoon of the 9th. Sponsors were Pastor Lemcke, Paul Finck, and Mrs. Finck.

Up to this point those baptized have been reported.

1764

Abdi, Thomas Schweighofer's Negro boy, was born in the night before Jan. 12, 1764, and baptized on the 14th. Sponsors were the two owners of the child.

Christian, son of Johann Georg Schneider and Barbara his wife, was born in the night before Jan. 20, 1764, and baptized the same day. Sponsors were Georg Faul and Rebecca his wife, whose place was represented by Mrs. Anna Barbara Rabenhorst.

Maria Magdalena, daughter of David Steiner and his wife Anna Margaretha, was born Jan. 21, 1764, before day and baptized in the afternoon. Sponsors: Samuel Kraus, Judith Flerl, and Mrs. Schweiger.

David, son of Joh. Gugel and his wife Anna Maria, was born Jan. 21 in the evening, and baptized on the 22nd after morning worship. Sponsors were Christoph Kraemer, his wife, and Zimmerebener.

Christian, son of Joh. Justus Gravenstein and his wife Catharina, was born Feb. 3, 1764, in the evening and received lay baptism soon after birth, which was confirmed on Feb. 4th. The witnesses of the lay baptism were Mrs. Kronberger, the child's father, Christian Bidenbach and his wife, and Mrs. Metzcher, who also baptized the child. Sponsors were the glazier Buntz and his wife and Joh. Michel.

Nathanael, son of Johannes Schneider and Catharina his wife, was born Feb. 11, 1764, and baptized the same day. Sponsors were Samuel Krause and Judith his wife and Ruprecht Zimmerebener.

David, child of G. Schleich and Maria Magd. his wife, was born Feb. 12, 1764, and baptized on the same day. Sponsors were Gabriel Maurer and Anna his wife and Ludwig Eigel.

Judith, daughter of Nicolaus Schubtrein and his wife Anna Maria, was born Feb. 15, 1764, early and baptized on the same day. Sponsors were Jos. Schubtrein, Maria his wife, and Judith Krause.

Josua, son of Martin Taescher and his wife Ursula, was born Feb. 16, 1764, and baptized the same day. Sponsors were Pastor Boltzius and his wife and John Adam Treutle.

Catharina, a Negro girl on Mr. Kiefer's plantation, was born March 5, 1764, and baptized on the 10th. Sponsors were Mr. Kiefer and his wife.

Dorothea, daughter of Schoolmaster Heck and his wife, was born at daybreak on March 31, 1764, and baptized on the afternoon of the same day. Sponsors were Zimmerebner, Mrs. Kiefer, and J. G. Buntz's wife.

Elieser, a Negro boy on Mr. Rabenhorst's plantation, was born at daybreak on March 11, 1764, at night and baptized in the afternoon of the 14th of March. Sponsors were Mr. Rabenhorst and his wife.

Catharina, daughter of Balthasar Rieser and his wife Maria, was born in the night before April 3, 1764, and baptized on the same day. Sponsors were Mrs. Boltzius and Master Kiefer and his wife.

Elisha, son of Thomas Schweighofer and Hanna his wife, was born April 8, 1764, and baptized on the 9th. Sponsors were Ruprecht Zimmerebener and Elisabeth Kogler.

Maria, daughter of Christian Steiner and Dorothea his wife, was born April 9, 1764, and baptized the same day. Sponsors were Ruprecht Zimmerebener, Maria Schubtrein, and Anna Marg. Steiner.

Johann Georg, son of Joh. Philip Paulitsch and his wife, was born April 12, 1764, and baptized the 13th. Sponsors were Johannes Hangleiter and Ursula his wife and Georg Gnann and his wife.

Maria, daughter of Joh. Georg Buntz and his wife, was born April 13th early, and baptized the same day. Sponsors were Georg Gnann, Mrs. Michler, and Angelica Oechsle.

Jonathan, child of Joh. Georg Pechtle and his wife Eva Barbara, was born June 19, 1764, early, and was baptized the same day. Sponsors were Pastor Boltzius, Mr. Treutlen, and his wife.

Maria Friederica, child of Johannes Rentz and his wife Barbara, was born July 11, 1764, and baptized on the 12th. Sponsors were Mrs. Lemcke, Zimmerebener, and Mrs. Faul.

Catharina, a Negro girl purchased by Mr. Treutlen, somewhat over three years old, was baptized July 30, 1764, when he and his wife took the place of sponsors.

Johann Martin, son of Johann Martin Rheinlaender and his wife Fridrica Catharina, was born Aug. 31, 1764, and baptized Sept. 1st. Sponsors were Christoph Kraemer and his wife, Pastor Boltzius, and his daughter Cath. Maria.

Salomo, son of Georg Gruber and his wife Elisabeth, was born Sept. 13, 1764, and baptized the following day in Jerusalem Church. Sponsors were Johann Justus Gravenstein and his wife, Jacob Mohr, Jun., and Mrs. Paulus.

David, son of Jacob Gnann and his wife Marg., was born in Bethany on Sept. 28 very early and was baptized on the same day. Sponsors were Zimmerebener, Faul, and his wife.

Israel, son of Johann Pflueger and his wife Barbara, was born Aug. [left unfilled], 1764, and baptized in Zion Church. Sponsors were Brandner, Heckel, and Cath. Zittrauer.

Maria, daughter of Johann Adam Treutlen, was born Nov. 16, 1764 early before day and baptized in the afternoon of the 17th. Sponsors were Master Johann Theobald Kieffer, his wife, and Mrs. Gertraud Boltzius.

Sarah, Joh. Michel's Negro girl, was born in the night between Nov. 14 and 15, 1764, and baptized on the 20th. Maria Michel and her son took the place of sponsors.

Maria, daughter of Conrad Rahn and his wife Anna Barbara, was born Dec. 2, 1764, in the afternoon and baptized in the forenoon of the 3rd. Sponsors were Joseph Schubtrein and his wife Maria.

Onesimus, Negro boy of Hangleiter's Negress, was born Dec. 8, 1764, and baptized on the 18th. Sponsors were the owners.

N. B. — Up to this point those baptized have been reported.

Georg, son of Joh. Casper Waldhauer and his wife Agnes, was born Dec. 27 and baptized Dec. 28, 1764. Sponsors were Joh. C. Wertsch and wife and Andrew Seckinger.

1765

David, child of Johann Jacob Metzcher and Margaretha his wife, was born Jan. 15, 1765, and baptized on the 16th. Sponsors were Mr. Joh. Caspar Wertsch and his wife Hanna Elisabeth, John Paulus, and his wife.

Immanuel, son of Joh. Georg Ziegler and his wife Catharina, was born Jan. 21, 1765 early, and baptized the 22nd. Sponsors were David Steiner, Joh. G. Haid, and Anna Maria Flerl.

Timotheus, son of Joh. Martin Greiner and his wife Maria, was born Feb. 2, 1765 very early and baptized in the afternoon of the same day in Zion Church. Sponsors were Master Wertsch, Mackh in Goshen, and Mrs. Lackner.

Salome, daughter of Georg Weber and his wife, was born April 3, 1765, and baptized the 4th. Sponsors were Mr. Wertsch and his wife and Maria Flerl.

Maria, daughter of Christian Birck and his wife, was born April 20, 1765, and baptized on the following Sunday. Sponsors were Ruprecht Zimmerebener, Mrs. Wertsch, and Mrs. Pastor Boltzius.

Joh. Paul Mueller's wife bore a dead child on 19 April 1765.

Georg, child of Georg Fischer and Maria his wife, was born may 19, 1765, in Bethany and baptized in the afternoon of the same day. Sponsors were Mr. Wertsch and Mrs. Finck.

Heinrich Ludwig, son of Joh. Georg Gravenstein and his wife Cath., was born May 21, 1765, and baptized on the 22nd. Sponsors were Ludwig Buntz, his wife, and John Michel.

Georg, a Negro boy who was born June 15, 1765, was baptized on the 19th, when the owners, namely Pastor Heinrich Lemcke and his wife, acted as sponsors.

Abiel, son of Johann Georg Haid and Eleonora his wife, was born June 27 before day, and baptized on the 28th. Sponsors were John Flerl, Sen. and his wife Mary, and Johann Georg Ziegler.

David, son of Michael Rieser and his wife Apollonia, was born in the night between July 8 and 9, 1765, and baptized in the forenoon of the 9th. Sponsors were Mr. Kieffer, Mrs. Mayer, Mr. Wertsch, and his wife.

Jacob, son of Joseph Schubtrein and Maria his wife, was born July 12, 1765 in the evening and baptized on the following day. Sponsors were Conrad Rahn, Nicol. Schubtrein, and his wife.

Hanna, daughter of Joh. Georg Schneider and his wife Barbara, was born July 12 and baptized on the 13th, 1765. Sponsors were Georg Faul and his wife Rebecca.

Friedrich, son of Friedrich Rester and his wife Maria Margareta, was born in Purysburg Township, May 16, 1765, and baptized July 22 in Jerusalem Church. Sponsors were Master Wertsch and his wife.

Margareta, daughter of Nicolai Winckler and his wife Anna Barbara, was born in Purysburg Township, May 15, 1765, and baptized there July 23rd. Sponsors were Georg Stuckardt and Marg. his wife, and Anna Maria, the wife of Ludwig Winckler.

Heinrich, son of Jacob Strohbart and his wife Maria Catherina, was born July 19, 1765 in Purysburg Township and baptized there on the 23rd. Sponsors were Ottilie Mengersdorff and her son Johann Georg Mengersdorff and Heinrich Chendrow.

Hanna Margareta, daughter of Isr. Leimberger and his wife Apol., was born July 25, 1765, and baptized before evening. Sponsors were Joh. Adam Treutle, his wife, and Hanna Elisabeth Flerl.

Michael, son of Gabriel Maurer and his wife Anna, was born Aug. 26, 1765, and baptized the same day. Sponsors were Carl Siegmund Ott and his wife.

The Negress of Flerl, Jun. or Brandner gave birth on Sept. 4 to a boy who was baptized Sept. 11, and died the same day. Sponsors were G. Zittrauer and his wife.

Agatha, daughter of Joh. Hangleitner and his wife Ursula, was born Sept. 23, 1765 in the evening at 10 o'clock, and baptized on the 24th. Sponsors were Master Joh. Casp. Wertsch and his wife Hanna Elisabeth and Mrs. Landfelder.

Jedidja, son of Ludwig Weitmann and his wife Anna Eva, was born Sept. 24, 1765, and baptized on the 25th. Sponsors were Pastor Lemcke and his wife.

David, son of Joh. Heinle and his wife Maria, was born early on Sept. 28, 1765, and baptized on the same day. Sponsors were G. Faul and his wife Rebecca.

Maria Magdalena, daughter of Daniel Schubtrein and his wife Magdalena, was born in the night before Oct. 5, 1765, and baptized the same day. Sponsors were Christoph Kraemer and his wife, Paul Mueller, Sen., and his wife.

Adam, Mr. Kieffer's Negro child, was born on his plantation Oct. 15, 1765, and baptized on the 17th in Jerusalem Church. Sponsors were Mr. Kieffer, the owner, and his daughter Elisabeth.

Daniel, son of Johannes Remshardt and his wife Anna Margaretha, was born Oct. 26, 1765, and baptized on the 27th. Sponsors were Samuel Kraus and Judith his wife.

Hanna, a Negro girl on Mr. von Muench's land, was born Oct. 26, 1765, and baptized on the 30th. Sponsors were Mr. Christian von Muench and his wife, who were represented by Mrs. Lemcke and John Scheraus.

Moses, child of an Englishman, Arthur Royal and Anna his wife, was born Dec. 13, 1764, and baptized Nov. 7, 1765 in Jerusalem Church. Sponsors were the parents, also the grandmother Anna Christiana Baill.

Johannes, a Negro child belonging to David Steiner, was born Nov. 11, 1765, in the night and baptized the same day. Sponsors were David Steiner and Anna Margareth his wife.

Matth. Bidenbach's wife gave birth to a stillborn boy, Nov. 26, 1765.

N. B. — Up to this point those baptized have been reported to the Society.

Johannes, Schweiger's Negro child, was born Dec. 10, 1765, and baptized on the 11th. Sponsors were Schweiger and his wife Margaretha.

Judith, daughter of young Flerl and his wife Hanna Elisabeth, was born Dec. 25, 1765, and baptized on the 26th. Sponsors were Samuel Kraus and Judith his wife.

1766

Salome, daughter of Samuel Kraus and Judith his wife, was born Jan. 3, 1766 in the preceding night and baptized on this day. Sponsors were David Steiner and Anna Marg. his wife.

Phoebe, Hangleiter's Negro girl, was born Jan. [left unfilled], 1766, and baptized on the 11th. Sponsors were Joh. Hangleiter and his wife.

Obadja, son of Joh. Georg Pechtle and his wife Eva Barbara, was born Jan. 29, 1766, and baptized on the 30th. Sponsors were Mr. Joh. Ad. Treutle and his wife, also Joh. Jacob Kronberger.

Johannes, Joseph Schubtrein's Negro boy, was born Jan. 30, 1766, and baptized. Sponsors were Jos. Schubtrein and his wife Maria.

Christian, a Negro boy, born on Mr. Rabenhorst's plantation, Jan. 14, 1766, was baptized on the 17th.

Simeon and Judith, Negro twins, were born Jan. 18th on Mr. Rabenhorst's land and baptized the same day. Mr. Rabenhorst and his wife were sponsors for these three children.

Obadja, son of Thomas Schweighofer and Hanna his wife, was born Feb. 4, 1766, and baptized. Sponsors were Ruprecht Zimmerebener, Joh. Georg Zittrauer, and Elisabeth Kogler.

Gideon, son of Joh. Mart. Paulitsch and his wife, was born Feb. 4, 1766 in the evening and baptized on the 5th. Sponsors were Joh. Casp. Wertsch and Rottenberger, who were represented by Daniel Schubtrein and Jac. Metzcher, and Mrs. Boltzius.

Judith, Mr. Kiefer's Negro girl, was born Jan. 29, 1766, and baptized Feb. 6. Mr. Kiefer and his daughter Hanna were sponsors.

Hanna Elisabeth, daughter of Joh. Klein and his wife Christiana, was born in the night before Feb. 11, 1766, and baptized the same day. Sponsors were Joh. Gugel, the wife of Jac. Gnann, and Mrs. Deininger.

David, son of David Steiner and his wife A. Marg., was born Feb. 20, 1766, early towards 3 o'clock and was baptized the same day.

Salome, a Negro girl, was born Feb. 22, 1766, and baptized the 26th. Sponsors were Pastor Lemcke and his daughter, Joh. Christiana.

Hanna, daughter of Mr. Treutle and his wife, was born Feb. 26, 1766 in the night, and baptized the same day. Sponsors were Joh. Jac. Kronberger, Mrs. Boltzius, and Mrs. Wertsch.

Johannes, son of Johannes Gruber and his wife Maria Magdalena, was born March 4, 1766, and baptized the same day. Sponsors were John Flerl, Jun., and Hanna Elisabeth his wife.

Lydia, daughter of Lucas Ziegler and his wife Salome, was born on Jubilate Sunday, April 20, 1766, and baptized the same day. Sponsors were G. Faul and Rebecca his wife, and Agnes Waldhauer.

N. B. — Young Mrs. Fetzer gave birth to a daughter on June 12, 1766, which died immediately after receiving lay baptism.

N. B. — Mrs. Rentz gave birth to a stillborn daughter, June 30, 1766.

Johann Gottlieb, child of Joh. Georg Zittrauer and his wife Catharina, was born July 8, 1766, and baptized the same day. Sponsors were Mr. Treutle, Mr. Wertsch, and his wife.

Johann Jacob, son of Joh. Martin Greiner and Maria his wife, was born in the night before July 28, 1766, and baptized the same day. Sponsors were Johann Casp. Wertsch and Jacob

Mackh in Abercorn, who was represented by Isr. Leimberger and Cath. Barb. Lackner.

Salome, daughter of Nicol. Schubtrein and his wife Anna Maria, was born July 30, and baptized on the 31st. Sponsors were S. Kraus and his wife Judith, also M. Schubtrein.

Nathan, a Negro boy, was born Aug. 7, 1766, and baptized on the 8th. Sponsors were the owners, namely, Pastor Lemcke and his wife.

David, son of Johannes Pflueger and his wife Barbara, was born Aug. 27, 1766, and baptized on the 28th. Sponsors were Joh. Georg Heckel, John Georg Zittrauer, and Catharina his wife.

Jacob, son of Jacob Gnann and his wife Margaretha, was born Sept. 21, the 17th Sunday after Trinity, and baptized on the 22nd. Sponsors were Ruprecht Zimmerebener, Georg Faul, and Rebecca his wife. In their absence they were represented by Andr. Seckinger, Caspar Waldhauer, and Elisabeth Margareta Kronberger.

Heinrich Ludwig, son of Urban Buntz and his wife, was born Sept. 23, 1766, and baptized on the 24th. Sponsors were Ruprecht Zimmerebener, represented by his son-in-law David Steiner, and Ludwig Buntz and Mrs. H. E. Wertsch.

Maria, daughter of Joh. Georg Deininger and his wife Anna Barbara, was born Sept. 27, late about 10, and baptized the 28th, 1766. Sponsors were Joh. Paulus and his wife, also Mrs. Rahn.

Christiana, child of Johann Georg Buntz and his wife Barbara, was born early on Oct. 4, 1766, and baptized the same day. Sponsors were Christ. Bidenbach, the wife of Ludwig Buntz, and the wife of G. Gnann.

Anna Margareta, daughter of Ludwig Winckler and his wife Anna Maria, resident in Purysburg, was born July 10, 1766, and baptized Oct. 15th. Sponsors were Friedrich Rester and his wife Margareta.

Daniel, daughter (sic) of Matthias Gugel and his wife, was born in the night before Nov. 2, 1766, and baptized on this day. It was the 23rd Sunday after Trinity. Sponsors were Zimmerebener [left unfilled].

Maria, daughter of Joh. Gravenstein and his wife Catharina, was born Nov. 4, 1766, in the evening and baptized on the 6th. Sponsors were Ludwig Buntz and his wife.

Salome, daughter of Joh. Georg Schneider and his wife Barbara, was born Aug. 21, 1766, and baptized the same day. Sponsors were the blacksmith Faul and his wife.

Bartholomeus, child of Daniel Mollet and his wife Mary, was born Oct. 20, 1766, in Purysburg, and baptized Nov. 12, 1766. Sponsors were the father himself, now a widower, and Rudolph Peninger and his wife.

Friedrich, son of Patrick Onyl [O'Neal] and his wife, was born Nov. 8, 1766, and baptized on the 9th. Mrs. Mich. Rieser had given him lay baptism, which was confirmed by Mr. Rabenhorst in the presence of Schleich, his wife, and the just mentioned Mrs. Rieser. He soon died on Nov. 10th and was quietly buried.

Johann Christoph, son of Mr. G. Ludwig Roth and his wife, was born in the night between Dec. 8 and 9, 1766, and baptized on the 10th. Sponsors were Mr. Chr. Kraemer and his wife.

Sulamith, Simon Reuter's Negro girl, was born Dec. 20, 1766, and baptized the same day. Sponsors were the owner and Dorothea Reuter.

1767

Anna Maria, daughter of Gregorius Stierle and his wife Maria Rosina, was born in Purysburg, Oct. 20, 1766, and baptized Feb. 2, 1767 in Ebenezer. Sponsors were Pininger and A. M. Winckler.

Elisabeth, daughter of Joh. Georg Gruber and his wife Elisabeth, was born between Feb. 4 and 5, 1767, and baptized on the 5th. Sponsors were Christ. Bidenbach and his daughter Catharina Gravenstein, Jacob Mohr, Jun., and Mrs. M. U. Paulus.

Johannes, son of Joh. Schneider and his wife Catharina, was born Dec. 29, 1766, early and was baptized the same day. Sponsors were Ruprecht Zimmerebener, Samuel Kraus, and Judith his wife.

Salomo, son of Ludwig Weitman and his wife, was born early on the morning of Feb. 11, 1767, and baptized on the same day. Sponsors were Pastor Lemcke and his wife.

Anna Margareta, daughter of Conrad Rahn and his wife, was born Feb. 19, 1767, in the evening, and baptized on the 20th. Sponsors were Joseph Schubtrein and Maria his wife.

Catharina, daughter of Johannes Remshardt and his wife Anna Marg., was born in the night between Feb. 19 and 20, 1767, and baptized the same day. Sponsors were Samuel Kraus and Judith his wife.

Hanna, daughter of Casper Waldhauer and his wife Agnesia, was born April 1, 1767, and baptized on the 2nd. Sponsors were Mr. J. C. Wertsch and his wife and Mrs. Ewen of Savannah.

On April 2, 1767, Mrs. Taescher gave birth to a stillborn son.

Johannes, son of Casper Heck and his wife Anna, was born April 3, 1767, and baptized the same day. Sponsors were Michler, J. Georg Buntz, and Marg. Kalcher.

Jacob, Zittrauer's Negro boy, was born April 18, 1767, and received on the 19th into the bosom of the Christian Church by baptism.

Johann Christoph, son of John Martin Rheinlander and his wife Friederica, was born in the night between July 14 and 15, 1767, and baptized on the 16th. Sponsors were Mr. Treutle,

Christopher Kraemer, and his wife, and Miss Cath. Marg. Boltzius.

Elieser, Johannes Hangleiter's Negro child, was born July 26, 1767, and baptized on the 27th. Hangleiter and she were sponsors.

Catherina, daughter of Joh. Georg Ziegler and his wife, was born Aug. 25, 1767, and baptized the same day. Sponsors were David Steiner, who was represented by Zimmerebener and Anna Margareta Steiner.

Mattheus, son of Georg Fischer and his wife Mary, was born Sept. 6, 1767, and baptized on the 8th. Sponsors were Johann C. Wertsch, Paul Finck, and his wife.

Maria, daughter of Johannes Flerl and his wife Hanna Elisabeth, was born in the night before Sept. 19, 1767, and baptized on the same day. Sponsors were Johann Flerl and Judith Kraus.

Anna Maria, daughter of Johann Georg Pechtle and his wife Eva Barbara, was born Sept. 27, 1767, and baptized the 28th. Sponsors were Joh. Michler and his wife and Mrs. Metzcher.

Anna Margaretha, daughter of Matth. Bidenbach and his wife, was born Sept. 27, 1767 towards evening and baptized the 28th. Sponsors were Joh. Hangleiter and his wife and the wife of Georg Gnann.

1768

Israel, son of Nicolaus Schubtrein and Anna Maria his wife, was born in the night between Aug. 23 and 24, 1768, and baptized the 24th. Sponsors were Joseph Schubtrein, who was represented by Israel Leimberger, and Maria Schubtrein, the wife of the aforementioned Joseph Schubtrein.

Hanna, daughter of Johannes Lastinger and his wife Anna Barbara, was born Aug. 25, 1768, and baptized the same day.

Sponsors were Friedrich Lackner and Johanna Christiana Lackner.

Salomo, son of Johann Jacob Kiefer and Dorothea his wife, was born and baptized Aug. 29, 1768. Sponsors were Salomo Zant and his wife Elisabeth and David Steiner.

Johann Ludwig Weitmann's wife gave birth to a stillborn daughter, Sept. 14, 1768. May God comfort both parents.

Josua, son of Johann Gugel and his wife Anna Maria, was born Sept. 28, 1768, and baptized the 29th. Sponsors were Ruprecht Zimmerebener, Christoph Kraemer, and his wife.

Agnesia, daughter of Lucas Ziegler and Salome his wife, was born Sept. 27, 1768, and baptized the 29th. Sponsors were Georg Faul and Rebecca his wife and Agnes, the wife of Caspar Waldhauer.

(Note by translator. — From now on some of the entries are in English. They are copied here as they occur.)

Thomas, son of Josias Dickson & his Wife, was born the 12th of Feb., 1768 at Hogeechy & was baptized the 13th of Octobr., 1768. The Mother only became Surety as the Father was unwell. (in English)

Sarah, Daughter of Aaron More & Grace his Wife, was born the 21st of June, 1768, & baptized the 17th of Octobr., 1768. The Parents themselves are Sureties. (in English)

Johannes, a Negro boy born to Simon Reuter, was baptized Nov. 9, 1768. Simon Reuter and his daughter Hanna served as sponsors. (in English)

Sarah, Daughter of Charles Hudson & his Wife Mary, was born the 30th Day of Aug. in the Parish of St. Matthew in the Year 1768, & baptized the 10th of Novr., 1768. The Mother only was present as a Godmother. (in English)

Randolph, son of Philip Singleton & his Wife Nancy, is born the 6th of Nov., 1768, & baptized on the first Day of Decr. Godfather was Benjamin Waston & the Mother aforenamed Mother of the Child. (in English)

Maria Margaretha, child of Johann Georg Zittrauer and his wife Catharina, was born and baptized Dec. 2, 1768. Sponsors were Mr. Johann Caspar Wertsch, represented by Samuel Kraus, and his wife Hanna Elisabeth and Miss Friedericke Maria Gronau.

Judith, daughter of Johann Remshardt and Anna Margareth his wife, was born Dec. 10, 1768, and baptized the 11th. Sponsors were Samuel Kraus and Judith his wife and Maria Magdalena Gruber.

Up to this point the number has been reported.

Margareth, a Negro girl belonging to the children of Kiefer, was born Dec. 10, 1768, and baptized the 22nd. Sponsors were Salomo Zant and his wife Elisabeth.

William, Son of Clement Martin, Esqr. and Mrs. Elizabeth Jackson, is born the 13th of Novr., 1768 at Abercorn & baptized the 27th Decr., 1768. The Parents stood Godfather & Godmother. (in English)

John, Son of Nicolaus Horton & Polly Goepel, is born the 12th of Novr., 1768 & baptized on the 31st of Decr., 1768. Godfather stood Thomas Lloyd for William Wylly & Nicols. Horton for John Stirck & the Mother of the Child stood Godmother. (in English)

1769

Johannes, son of Georg Gruber and Elisabeth his wife, was born in the night between Jan. 24 and 25, 1769, and baptized the 26th. Sponsors were Johann Gravenstein and Catharina his wife, Jacob Mohr, and Ursula Paulus.

Salomon, son of Johann Gruber and his wife Maria Magdalena, was born Jan. 25, 1769, and baptized the 26th. Sponsors were Samuel Kraus and Judith his wife.

William Ewen, son of Jacob Caspar Waldhauer and Agnes his wife, was born Jan. 24, 1769, and baptized the 26th. Sponsors were Johann Caspar Wertsch and his wife Hanna Elisabeth and Johann Ulrich Neidlinger.

Catharina, daughter of Johann Maurer and Maria Magdalena his wife, was born Feb. 1, 1769, and baptized the 2nd. Sponsors were Salomo Zant and Elisabeth his wife and Hanna Elisabeth Flerl.

Jojada, a Negro child, was born to the Lemcke relationship Feb. 5th, and baptized on the 8th. Timotheus Lemcke and Johanna Lemcke were sponsors.

Lydia, daughter of David Steiner and Anna Margareth his wife, was born and baptized March 5, 1769. Sponsors were Samuel Kraus and Judith his wife and Anna Margareth Schweiger.

Margareth, daughter of Matthaeus Weinkauf and Christina his wife, was born March 1, 1769, and baptized the 5th. Sponsors were Peter Freiermuth and Anna Catharina Groll.

Margareth, daughter of Bartholomaeus Spring and Anna his wife, was born Jan. 30, 1768, and baptized March 5, 1769. Sponsors were Daniel Zettler and Catharine Lane.

Johann Friedrich, son of Friedrich Ochs and his wife Anna, was born March 11, 1769, and baptized the same day. Sponsors were Christiana Steiner, David Steiner, and Sibylla Staeheli.

Daniel, son of Johann Martin Rheinlaender and Friedericka Catharina his wife, was born March 16, 1769, and baptized on the 21st. Hanna Margaret, the wife of Christoph Kraemer, Daniel Burgsteiner, and Catharine Margaret Neidlinger were sponsors.

Dorothea, daughter of Jacob Gnann and Maria Margareth his wife, was born March 23, 1769, and baptized on the 24th. Sponsors were Ruprecht Zimmerebener, Rebecca Faul, and Anna Juliana Schmid.

Elisabeth, daughter of Thomas Schweighofer and Hanna his wife, was born in the night before March 25, 1769, and baptized on the 25th. Sponsors were Ruprecht Zimmerebener, Judith Kraus, and Elisabeth Kogler.

Sophia, Daughter of Townsend Robinson & his Wife Sophia, was born on the 17th of May, 1768, & was baptized the 31st of March, 1769. The Parents both stood Godfather. (in English)

David, Son of Peter Stiedler & his Wife, was born on the [left unfilled] of Octobr., 1768, & was baptized the 9th of April, 1768 (sic). The Father stood Godfather & Anna Paulus stood Godmother. (in English)

Maria, daughter of Johannes Oexlin and Elisabeth his wife, was born April 21, 1769, and baptized the same day. Sponsors were Lucas Ziegler and Barbara Deininger.

Johanna, daughter of Joh. Hangleiter and Ursula his wife, was born in the night of June 8, 1769, and baptized on the same day. Sponsors were Mr. Caspar Wertsch and his wife Hanna Elisabeth besides Mrs. Friedericka Maria Triebner.

Rachel, daughter of Ulrich Geiger and his wife Apollonia, was born beyond the Hogeechy River in the month of Feb., 1769, and baptized on June 13th. Sponsors were Friedrich Rester and his wife Margareth.

Johann Justus Gravenstein, son of Johann Justus Gravenstein and his wife Catharina, was born June 13, 1769, and baptized the same day. Sponsors were Johan Michel and his wife Maria besides [left unfilled].

Salome Scheeraus, daughter of Johann Scheeraus and his wife Anna Maria, was born June 19, 1769, and baptized the same day. Sponsors were Ludwig Weidman and his wife Anna Eva and Elisabeth Mohr.

Johann Ulrich Fezer was born July 17, 1769, and baptized on the 18th. The parents are Johann Ulrich Fezer and his wife Johanna. Sponsors were John Ulrich Neidlinger and his wife Waldpurga and Johann Scheeraus.

Samuel, Son of John Teal & his Wife Ruth, was born the 6th of June, 1769, & baptized on the 24th of July a. d. Godfather stood the Father himself. (in English)

Fanny, Daughter of James Dupuis & Fancy [sic] his Wife, born in Carolina the 30th of March, 1768, & baptized the 24th of July, 1769. The parents themselves were Sureties for the Child. (in English)

Christopher, Son of Edward Teal & his Wife Rebecca, born the 24th of March, 1764 in Carolina, was baptized the 24th of July, 1769. (in English)

Sally, Daughter of the forementioned Parents, born on the 5th Decembr, 1761, baptized the 24th of July, 1769. (in English)

James, Son of the just mentioned Parents, was born 24th Octobr., 1769, & baptized the 24th July, 1769. The Parents stood Godfather & Godmother for these tree [sic] Children just successively mentioned. (in English)

Drury Scraggs was born in the month of Sept. 1768, and baptized Aug. 3, 1769. The parents and likewise sponsors are Drury Scraggs and Thomas Howell and Elisabeth Howell. (in English)

Philip Howell, son of Thomas Howell and his wife Elisabeth, was born Nov. 10, 1767, and baptized Aug. 3, 1769. Sponsors were the father, Thomas Howell, Martin Dasher, and Ursula Dasher.

Jonathan Pflueger, son of Johannes Pflueger and his wife Barbara, was born Aug. 6, 1769, and baptized the 7th. Sponsors were David Unselt and his wife Anna, Georg Heckel, and Anna Barbara Deininger.

Joseph Rahn, son of Conrad Rahn and his wife Anna Barbara, was born Aug. 9, 1769 in the night and baptized the same day 1769. Sponsors were Joseph Schubtrein and his wife Maria.

Anna Maria Buntz, daughter of Johann Georg Buntz and his wife Barbara, was born Sept. 2, 1769, and baptized the same day. Sponsors were Johann Christ. Bittenbach, Maria Muehler, and Anna Gnann.

Elizabeth Thomas, Gilshott Thomas and his Wifs Daughter, was born the 11 Feb., 1769, and baptized the 15 Sept., 1769. Godfathers and Godmothers are both parents and Johann Caspar Wertsch. (in English)

Johannes Floerl was born Sept. 3, 1769, and baptized the next day. The parents are Johann Floerl and his wife Hanna Elisabeth. The sponsors were Christoph Friedrich Triebner and his wife Frederica Maria Triebner.

Anna Catharine Fischer, daughter of Georg Fischer and his wife Maria, was born Sept. 24, 1769, and baptized the following Sept. 25. Sponsors were Joh. Caspar Wertsch, Paul Finck, and his wife Anna Margaretha Finck.

Benaja Zant, son of Salmo Zant and his wife Elisabeth, was born Oct. 1, 1769, and baptized the same day. Sponsors were Christoph Friedrich Triebner, Friedericha Maria Triebner, and Johann Jacob Kronenberger.

Friedrich Wilhelm Mueller, son of Joh. Paul Mueller and his wife Elisabeth, was born Oct. 1, 1769, and baptized on the 2nd. Sponsors were Christoph Triebner, Friederika Triebner, and Salomo Zant.

Christiana Candace, daughter of Mr. Rabenhorst's Negro Daniel and Anna our Negress, was baptized by me as the first heathen child, on the 22 Sunday after Trinity, Oct. 22, 1769, in my house. She was born Oct. 18th. Sponsors were I, Christoph Friedrich Triebner, and my wife Friederika Maria Triebner.

Salome, daughter of Israel Leimberger and his wife Apollonia, was born Nov. 2, 1769, and baptized the same day. Sponsors were Joseph Schubtrein, Agnesia Waldhauer, and Lucia Kronberger.

Johann Adam Freyermuth's and his wife Maria's son Johann Adam was born Nov. 23, 1769, and baptized the 24th. Sponsors were Johanna Christiana Lemcke, Joseph Schubtrein, and Assa Imanuel.

David, son of Georg Ziegler and his wife Anna Catharina, was born in the night before Nov. 27, 1769, and baptized on the 28th. Sponsors were Johannes Floerl, Sen., David Steiner, and his wife Anna Margaretha.

Samuel and Elizabeth, twins of Johann Heinle and Maria Barbara his wife, were born in the night before Dec. 8, 1769, and baptized the same day. Sponsors were David Steiner and Anna Margaretha his wife, Samuel Krauss, and his wife Judith.

Christina, daughter of Nicolaus Schubtrein and his wife, was born Dec. 29, 1769, and baptized on the 30th. Sponsors were Joseph Schubtrein and Maria his wife and Judith Krauss.

Up to this point the number has been reported.

1770

David Bechtele, son of Georg Bechtele and his wife, was born Jan. 11, 1770, and baptized on the 12th. Sponsors were Jacob Mezger and his wife and Johann Muehler and his wife Maria.

Catharina Maria, daughter of Johannes Rens and his wife Barbara, was born Jan. 11, 1770, and baptized on the 12th. Sponsors were Mrs. Catharina Lemcke, Friederica Maria Triebner, and Ruprecht Zimmerebener.

David Klein was born Jan. 17, 1770, and baptized the next day. The parents are Johann Klein and his wife Christina. Sponsors were Urban Bunz, [left unfilled] Deininger, and Margareth Gnan.

Elisabeth, daughter of Heinrich Meyer and Maria Franciska his wife, 5 years old, was born in the month of Sept., 1764, and baptized Jan. 30. 1770. Sponsors were David Unselt and his wife Anna and also Elisabeth Strohhacker.

David, son of Heinrich Meyer and his wife Maria Franciska, was born in the month of March, 1766, and baptized Jan. 30, 1770. Sponsors were David Unselt and his wife and Strohhacker.

Gideon Rosch, son of Abraham Rosch and his wife Hanna, was born Feb. 18, 1770, and baptized the same day. Sponsors were Elisabeth Croneberger, Jacob Croneberger, and Daniel Burcksteiner.

Johanna Frederika, daughter of Johann Leonhardt Niesse and his wife, was born March 9, 1770, and baptized March 10, the festival of commemoration and consecration of the new church after the morning worship. Sponsors were Christoph Friedrich Triebner and his wife Friederika Maria and Johanna Lemcke.

John, son of Christopher Hudson and his wife Sarah, was born Nov. 1, 1769, and baptized March 16, 1770. Sponsors were both parents.

William, son of [left unfilled] Wilson, was born [left unfilled], 1769, and baptized March 23, 1770 in the new Jerusalem Church. Sponsors were William Wilson and his wife Sarah.

David, son of Johann Friedrich Ochs and his wife, was born March 23, 1770, and baptized the next day. Sponsors were David Steiner and his wife along with Christian Steiner.

Elisabeth, a Negro girl belonging to Christian Steiner, was born March 6, 1770, and baptized on the 6th. Christian Steiner was sponsor.

Maria Catharina, daughter of Johann Schneider and his wife, was born April 7, 1770, and baptized on the 8th. Sponsors were Samuel Krauss and his wife Judith, along with Anna Margaret Steiner.

Johannes, son of Pertrico Niles, was born [left unfilled], 1769, and baptized April 16, 1770. Sponsors were Johann Caspar Wertsch, Elisabeth Margaretha Kronenberger, and the hatter Nessler.

Johanna, daughter of Ulrich Neidlinger and his wife, was born April 23, 1770, and baptized the next day. Sponsors were Ruprecht Zimmerebener, Anna Margaretha Schweiger, and Anna Maria Gugel.

Martha, David Steiner's Negro girl, was born May 3, 1770, and baptized the next day. Sponsors were David Steiner and his wife Anna Margaretha.

Agnesia, daughter of Johann Michel Bohrmann and his wife Maria Magdalena, was born May 11, 1770, and baptized on the 12th. Sponsors were Christoph Kraemer and his wife, and Caspar Waldhauer and his wife.

[left unfilled], daughter of Johann Paul Mueller, Jun. and his wife Anna, was born May 14, 1770, and baptized the same day. Sponsors were Salomo Zant and his wife Elisabeth and Hanna Kiefer.

Jacob Odem, son of Abraham Odem and his wife, was born Nov. 3, 1768, and baptized May 15, 1770. Sponsors were the parents and Mr. Johann Caspar Wertsch.

Margaretha, daughter of Christian Oechsle, Sen., and his wife, was born in the evening before May 19, 1770, and baptized May 20th. Sponsors were Urban Punz, Maria Michel, and Margaretha Neidlinger.

Johannes, son of Johann Martin Greiner and his wife Maria, was born Dec. 17, 1768, and baptized June 10, 1770. Sponsors were Johann Caspar Wertsch and Barbara Lackner.

Samuel, son of Johann Martin Greiner and his wife, was born Feb. 18, 1770 in Halifax and baptized here in Ebenezer, June 10, 1770. Sponsors were Johann Caspar Wertsch and Michael Buehner and his wife Maria.

Daniel Burcksteiner's wife gave birth to a stillborn son July 6, 1770.

Christoph August Gottlob, son of Christoph Friedrich Triebner, third minister here, and his wife Friederika Maria, was born Aug. 8, 1770 in the afternoon and on the next day dedicated to the Lord Christ by holy baptism. Sponsors were Mr. Johann Aug. Urlsperger in Augsburg, Johanna Christiana Lemcke, and Johann Caspar Wertsch.

Matthias, son of Joseph Schubdrein and Maria his wife, was born in the night before Aug. 11, 1770, and baptized on the 11th. Sponsors were Nicolaus Schubdrein and his wife Anna Maria and Conrad Rahn.

Johann Adam, son of Mr. Johann Adam Treutlen and Margaretha his wife, was born Aug. 29, 1770, and baptized on the 31st. Sponsors were Christian Rabenhorst and his wife Anna Barbara.

Samuel, son of Jacob Heinle and Christina his wife, was born Aug. 24, 1770, and baptized on the 25th. Sponsors were Samuel Kraus and his wife Judith.

Nannie, daughter of Friedrich Rosberg and Johanna his wife, was born in the night before Sept. 13, 1770, and baptized on the

16th. Both parents-in-law brought the child to the Lord Jesus by baptism.

Hanna, daughter of Johann Caspar Wertsch and his wife Elisabetha, was born Aug. 21, 1770, and on the same day united to the Lord Jesus by holy baptism by Mr. Johann Floerl, Sen. and Mrs. Friederika Maris Triebner as sponsors.

Elisabeth, daughter of Samuel Krauss and his wife, was born Sept. 27, 1770, and baptized the next day. Sponsors were David Steiner and Anna Margaretha his wife.

Daniel, son of Johann Peter Freyermuth and his wife A. Catharina, was born Oct. 10, 1770, and baptized on the 11th. Sponsors were Johann Heinrich Bunz, the wife of Johann Schiele, and Nicolaus Schubdrein and his wife.

Asa, son of Johann Remshardt and his wife, was born Oct. 13, 1770, and baptized the same day. Sponsors were Samuel Krauss and his wife Judith.

Hanna Elisabeth, daughter of Jacob Kiefer and his wife, was born Oct. 14, 1770, and baptized the same day. Sponsors were Salomo Zant and his wife Elisabeth.

Salome Steiner, daughter of David Steiner and his wife Anna Margaretha, was born Oct. 14, 1770, and baptized on the next night. Samuel Krauss and his wife Judith and Anna Margaretha Schweiger.

Christian, son of Christian Steiner and his wife, was born Oct. 16, 1770, baptized on Oct. 17th. Sponsors were Joseph Schubdrein and his wife and Ruprecht Zimmerebener.

Christina, daughter of Michael Rieser and his wife Apollonia, was born Oct. 27th, and baptized the next day. Sponsors were Johann Caspar Wertsch and his wife and Maria Friederika Triebner.

On Nov. 8, 1770 Sophia Thorn, 20 years old, wife of David Thorn, an Englishman, after previous examination was baptized here in my house together with her 10 months old child, Polly. Sponsors for the mother were her husband, and Johanna Lemcke, for the child both parents.

David, son of Arthur Royal and his wife, 4 months old, was baptized here in Jerusalem Church, Dec. 13, 1770. Sponsors were both parents.

Heinrich Ludwig, son of Johann Justus Gravenstein and his wife Catharina, was born Dec. 25 on Christmas eve and baptized on Christmas day. Sponsors were Johann Michel and his wife and Ludewich Punz and his wife.

1771

Phoebe, a Negro girl belonging to Mrs. Pastor Lemcke, was born Jan. 14, 1771, and baptized the next day. Sponsors were Mrs. Pastor Catharina Lemcke and Timotheus Lemcke.

Friedrich, son of Johann Scherraus, was born Oct. 13, 1770, and baptized on the 15th. Sponsors were John Michler and his wife Maria.

1772

William Hattin, Son of Richard Stafford and Mary his Wife, born on the 14th of Nov., 1770, and Baptized the 23th of Ap., 1772. Godfathers are both Parents. (in English)

David, son of Georg Gruber and his wife Elisabeth, was born April 23, 1772, and baptized the following day. Sponsors were Johann Justus Gravenstein and his wife, Jacob Mohr, who was represented by Ludewich Punz, and Ursula Paulus.

Johann Adam, son of Johann Adam Freyermuth and his wife Maria, was born in the night between May 8 and 9, and baptized the 9th, 1772. Sponsors were Joseph Schubtrein, Miss Johanna Lemcke, and Timotheus Lemcke.

[left unfilled], daughter of Joseph Schubtrein and Maria his wife, was born June 5, 1772, and baptized the same day. Sponsors were (left vacant).

Ester, Daughter of Robert Hudson and Mary his Wife, has been born on the 26th of Oct., 1771, and baptized on the 8th of June, 1772. Godfathers are both Parents. (in English)

Isaak, Son of Christopher Hudson and Sarah his Wife, born on the 2d of March, 1772, and baptized on the 9th of June, 1772. Godfathers are Richard Togged and both Parents. (in English)

Christian, son of Johann Martin Rheinlaender and his wife Friederika Catharina, was born June 17, 1772, early about 3 o'clock and baptized on the 18th. Sponsors were Christoph Kraemer and his wife, Daniel Burcksteiner, and Catharine Margaret Macai.

John, Son of Thomas Unterword and his Wife, born the 2d of Dec., 1768, baptized on the 4th of July, 1772. Witnesses are Mr. Martin Dasher & his Wife. (in English)

Ede, Daughter of Thomas Unterword and his Wife, born the 20th of Octobr., 1771, baptized the fourth of July, 1772. Godfathers Mr. Dasher and his Wife Ursula.

Johannes, son of Johann Scherraus and his wife Anna Maria, was born Aug. 7, 1772, and baptized the next day. Sponsors were Michael Haberer and his wife Anna Eva.

Bethsey, Daughter of Francis Win and his wife, born the 16th of Sept., 1771, baptized the 30th of May, 1772. Godfathers and Godmother are both Parents. (in English)

Josua, son of Salomo Zant and his wife, was born Sept. 1, 1772, and baptized on the 4th. Sponsors were Christoph

Friedrich Triebner and his wife Friederika Maria and Jacob Cronenberger.

Joh. Paul, son of Joh. Paul Miller and his wife, was born Sept. 1, and baptized the next day. Sponsors were Johann Floerl and his wife, Samuel Krauss and his wife.

Salome, daughter of Daniel Burcksteiner and his wife, was born Sept. 4, 1772, and baptized the next day. Sponsors were Martin Daescher, Sen., and his wife Ursula and also Elisabeth Daescher.

Josua, son of Johann Gruber in Ogeechee and his wife Maria Magdalena, was born Aug. 31, 1772, and baptized Oct. 25, 1772. Sponsors were Samuel Krauss and his wife and Johann Lastinger.

Maria, daughter of Johann Scheeraus and his wife Anna Maria Magdalena, was born Sept. 25, 1772, and received lay baptism the same day. Sponsors were Johann Michel and Maria his wife.

The above child on account of great weakness received lay baptism in the name of the triune God, but the baptism was confirmed by me.

Christian Friedrich Hekel, son of Johann Hekel and his wife Anna Margaretha, was born Oct. 4, 1772, and baptized the same day. Sponsors were Urban Bunz and his wife and Christoph Friedrich Triebner.

Christina, daughter of Johann Heinle and his wife Christina, was born Oct. 7, 1772, and baptized the next day. Samuel Krauss and his wife were sponsors.

William Makai, son of Charles Makai and his wife, was born Oct. 8, 1772, and baptized the same day. Sponsors were Salomo Zant and Elisabeth his wife and also Ulrich Neidlinger.

Martha, 3 years old, daughter of William Colson and his wife, was baptized Oct. 27, 1772, and on the same day committed beside her one year old, sister Sarah, to the Lord Jesus by the bath of holy baptism. Sponsors were both parents.

Ann, Daughter of Aquila Miles and Henrietta his Wifes, born the 9th of Sept., 1772, baptized the 1st of Nov., 1772. Parents were witnesses. (in English)

Jacob, son of Conrad Rahn, was born Nov. [left unfilled], 1772, and baptized the same day. Sponsors were Joseph Schubtrein and his wife.

Jacob, son of [left unfilled] Sauler in Ogeechee and his wife, was born and baptized Nov. 14, 1772. Sponsors were Jacob Meier and Mrs. Geiger.

Christian, son of Daniel Zettler and Hanna his wife, was born two months too early after Christian marriage Nov. 14, 1772, and baptized on the 16th. Johann Jacob Kroneberger, Christian Daescher, and Ursula Daescher were sponsors.

Margaret, daughter of Joh. Walter in Halifax and his wife Anna Catharina, was born July 10, 1772, and baptized Nov. 18, 1772. Sponsors were Nicol. Schubtrein and his wife.

Salome, daughter of Joh. Martin Greiner and his wife Mary, was born Aug. 8, 1772, and baptized on Dec. 9th. Sponsors were Johann Caspar Wertsch and his wife and Barbara Lackner.

So far the number reported 37.

1773

Joel, son of Johann Jacob Kiefer and his wife, was born in the night before Jan. 26, 1773, and baptized on the 27th. Sponsors were Simon Reuter, Salomo Zant, and Dorothea Kiefer.

Christian and Christina, a pair of twins, children of Johann Remshardt and his wife Margaretha, were born Jan. 30, 1773, and both received lay baptism the same day. The boy died half an hour afterwards.

Isaac and Mary, a pair of twins of Isaac Torth, 20 miles from here, were born Feb. 14th and received lay baptism on the 16th, 1773.

Christian, son of Johann Justus Gravenstein and his wife Catharina, was born May 7th and baptized on the 8th. Sponsors were Ludwig Bunz and Barbara his wife and Urban Bunz.

Sarah Trager, wife to Shadrit Harper, 16 year of Age, was baptized on the 5th of March, 1773. Witnesses were Daniel Burgsteiner and Maria his Wife. (in English)

Abraham, Son of [left unfilled] Ravot of Purrisburrow, 3 months old, was baptized the third of March, 1773. Godfathers were John Strohbarth in whose Place stood Mr. Dasher and both Parents. (in English)

Salome, a Negro child belonging to Johann Floerl, was born March [left unfilled], 1773, and baptized [left unfilled]. Sponsors were Johann Floerl and his wife.

Mary, a Negro child belonging to Salomo Zant, was born March 10, 1773, and baptized [left unfilled]. Sponsors were Salomo Zant and Apelone Rieser.

The children of Johann Heinle and David Steiner were not reported.

Georg, a Negro child belonging to Christina Kiefer, was born Jan. 10, 1773, and baptized March 24, 1773. Sponsors were Christina Kiefer and Salomo Zant.

Christian Steiner's son, was born May 6, 1773, and baptized the next day. Sponsors were Samuel Krauss and Ruprecht Zimmerrebner.

Mary Barbara, daughter of Mary Barbara Wobner, a woman from Switzerland, travelling through here, was born May 8, 1773, and baptized on the following Sunday. Sponsors were Jacob Meier and his wife and Ursula Daescher.

On May 11, 1773, the following eleven children were baptized in Mr. Bacon's house:—

Anne, 6 years old, and Clermont, 3 years old, both children of Joshua Stafford and his wife Martha. The parents were sponsors.

Sarah, 5 years old, Samuel, 3 years old, and David, 8 months old, all three children of Abraham Wiehle and his wife in Carolina. The parents were sponsors.

William, 6 years old, Susannah, 4 years old, and Anne, 2 years old, children of Samuel Wilkins and wife Mary. The parents were sponsors.

John, 5 years old, and Peter, 3 years old, children of Jacob Kettel and his wife Elizabeth. Sponsors were the parents themselves.

Martin, 3 years old, son of Martin Schuman and his wife Tabitha, was baptized together with the 10 children aforementioned on May 11, 1773. The parents were sponsors.

David, son of Joh. Bassinger in Ogeechee and his wife Barbara, was born March 24, 1773, and baptized May 18, 1773. Sponsors were Johann Floerl and Maria Magdalena Gruber.

[left unfilled], daughter of Christian Oechsle, Sen., was born in the night between July 14 and 15, 1773. Sponsors were Ulrich Neidlinger and his wife and Mary Michler. She was baptized on the 17th.

Sarah, daughter of an Englishman [left unfilled] Buts, 3 months old, was baptized July 18, 1773. Sponsors were both parents; the father was represented by [left unfilled].

Catharina, daughter of Nicolaus Schubtrein and his wife Margaretha, was born Aug. 15, 1773, and baptized the next day. Sponsors were Joseph Schubtrein and Agnesia his wife.

Salomo, son of Friedrich Schrempf and his wife Christiana Elisabeth, was born Aug. 16, 1773, and baptized the following day. Sponsors were Salomo Schrempf and his wife.

Catharina, daughter of Matthias Bittenbach and his wife Anna, was born Sept. 6, 1773, and baptized the same day. Sponsors were Johannes Hangleiter and Catharina Hangleiter.

John, son of Johannes Maurer and his wife Maria Magdalena, was born Sept. 6, 1773, and baptized the next day. Sponsors were Johann Flerl and his wife and Salomo Zant.

Johann Christoph, son of John Martin Reihlaender and his wife Friedrika, was born Oct. 3, 1773, and baptized on the 11th. Sponsors were Christoph Friedrich Triebner and his wife Friedrika Maria and Mr. Christoph Kraemer.

Anne, daughter of [left unfilled] Trowell, an Englishman, and his wife, was born Aug. 12 and baptized Oct. 16, 1773. Sponsors were Johann Lastinger and Barbara his wife.

Tobias, son of Peter Freyermuth, was born in the night between Dec. 7 and 8, 1773, and baptized on the 8th. Sponsors were Johann Caspar Wertsch, Ludwig Bunz, Anna Margaretha Knoll, and Anna Schiel.

Elisabeth, daughter of Jacob Gnan and his wife Hanna, was born Dec. 19, 1773 in the night and baptized the next day. Sponsors were Georg Gruber and his wife Elisabeth and Ludwig Bunz and his wife Barbara.

So far the number reported.

1774

Zacharias, Son of Robert Wilson and Rachel his Wife, was born on the 12th Day of April, 1771, baptized on the 7th of Jan., 1774. Godfathers were both Parents. (in English)

Lydia, Daughter of Charles Deal and his wife, was born the 6th of Jan., 1768, and baptized on the 7th of Jan., 1774. (in English)

Likewise Mary, Daughter of Charles Deal, born the 9th of Aug., 1774, and baptized the 7th of Jan., 1774. Godfathers were both Parents. (in English)

Anna Maria, daughter of John Scherauss and his wife Anna, was born Jan. 18, 1774, and baptized the next day. Sponsors were Michael Haberer and his wife Anna Eva, also the widow Elisabeth Meyer.

Johanna, daughter of Andreas Gnan and his wife Anna Franziska, was born April 8, 1774, and baptized the next day. Sponsors were Miss Johanna Christiana Lemcke, Salome Lemcke, and Timotheus Lemcke. The last named was represented by Johann Rittenberger.

W[left unfilled] William May and Mary his Wife's Daughter, born on the 30th of Sept., 1772, baptized on the 12th of April, 1774. Both Parents were Godfathers. (in English)

Susannah, a Negro child belonging to Mr. Nicolaus Cronenberger, was born April 12, 1774, and baptized the same day. Sponsors were Margareth Elisabeth Cronenberger and Elisabeth Cronenberger and also Nicolaus Cronenberger.

Jacob, son of Jacob Buehler and his wife Christiana Elisabeth, was born July 17, 1774, and baptized the same day. Sponsors: Timotheus Lemcke and Miss Johanna Lemcke, Catharina Gravenstein, and Joh. Adam Freyermuth.

Cornelius, son of [left unfilled] Geiger in Ogeechee and his wife, was born Feb. 1, 1774, and baptized July 18, 1774. Sponsors were Mr. Rister and his wife.

Sarah, Archibald Patterson and his Wife's daughter, is born in the month of April, 1772, and baptized the 6th Day of Aug. Godfathers both Parents. (in English)

Daniel, Son of Archibald Patterson and his Wifes Mary, is born the 10th of Dec., 1773, and baptized the 6th Day of Aug., 1774. Both Parents were Godfathers. (in English)

Maria Margaretha, daughter of Georg Zittrauer and his wife Catharina, was born May 6, 1774, early and baptized the same day. Sponsors were Friedrika Maria Triebner and Mr. Wertsch and his wife Elisabeth.

Israel, son of Johann Adam Freyermuth, was born of his wife Mary, early in the morning Aug. 17, 1774, and baptized on the same day. Sponsors were Timotheus Lemcke and Miss Johanna Lemcke and Mr. Jacob Buehler.

Christoph Friedrich, son of Georg Hekel and his wife Anna Margaretha, was born Sept. 19, 1774, and baptized the same day. Sponsors were Christoph Friedrich Triebner, Miss Johanna Lemcke, and Urban Bunz and his wife. Timotheus Lemcke represented Mr. Bunz.

Martha, Daughter of Lin Man and his Wife in Ogeechee, was born the 19th of March, 1774, and baptized the 19th of Sept., 1774. (in English)

John, Son of Bansamon Lanier and Eolef his Wifes, was born on the 1st of Dec., 1772, and baptized on the [left unfilled] of Oct., 1774. Godfather and Godmother both Parents. (in English)

Grace, Daughter of James Wilson and Sarah his Wife's, was born the 3d of Jan., 1772, and baptized on the 21st of Oct., 1774. Godfathers were both Parents. (in English)

Nathanael, Son of Louis Williams and his wife, was born in the year 1769 on the 26th of Jan. Christened on the 17th of Nov., 1774. (in English)

Louis, Son of Louis William and his wife, born the 2d of Feb., 1771, christened on the 17th of Nov., 1774. (in English)

Judith, Daughter of Louis William and his Wife, born on the 26th of March, 1773, christened the 17th of Nov., 1774. Both Parents stood witnesses for their three Children. (in English)

Davis, Son of Louis Margon, born the 18th of Sept., 1774, baptized the 27th of Nov., 1774. Godfathers were Mr. Wunderlich and John Louis Winkle from Purrysburgh. (in English)

Johanna Friederika, daughter of Johann Martin Reinlander and his wife, was born Nov. 11, 1774, and baptized Nov. 15, 1774. Sponsors were Christ. Fried. Triebner and his wife, Mr. Christoph Kraemer and his wife.

Christian and Samuel, twins of Israel Leimberger and his wife Apelone, born Dec. 2, and baptized the same day, 1774 by Mr. Sen. Muehlberg. Sponsors were Samuel Kra[left unfilled] and his wife and Agnesia Waldhauer.

Josua, son of Israel Kiefer and his wife Hanna Margareth, was born in the night between Dec. 2 and 3, 1774, and baptized on the 3rd. Sponsors were Johann Floerl and his wife.

Johann Christoph, son of Johann Christoph Kraemer and his wife Catharina, was born Dec. 21, 1774 in the evening about 7 o'clock, and baptized Dec. 22nd. Sponsors were Christoph Friedrich Triebner and his wife and Mr. Johann Hangleiter and his wife.

Elisabeth, Daughter of Mr. Benjamin Daley and his wife, was born on the 6th of Decr., 1774, and christened the 22nd of Dec., 1774. Both Parents were Godfathers. (in English)

Martha, Daughter of Richard Stephen, born in the Month of Feb., 1774, baptized on the 27th of Dec., 1774. Benjamin Daley and the Mother of this Child were Godfathers. (in English)

Dorothea, daughter of Joh. Martin Daescher and his wife Elisabeth, was born Dec. 28, 1774, and baptized the same day. Sponsors were Christian Daescher, Ursula Daescher, and Maria Buerkstein.

Johanna, daughter of Johann Caspar Greiner and his wife, was born Aug. 31, 1774, baptized Dec. 26, 1774. Sponsors were Christian Steiner and his wife Dorothea.

Catharina, daughter of David Steiner and Margareth his wife, was born Dec. 25, 1774, baptized the 26th. Samuel Krauss and his wife, Georg Schweiger and his wife were sponsors.

Salome, daughter of Joh. Jacob Heinle and his wife, was born Dec. 29, 1774, and baptized the same day. Sponsors: Samuel Krauss and his wife.

1775

Johann Friedrich, son of Joh. Fried. Lackner and his wife, was born Jan. 3, 1775, baptized on the 5th. Sponsors were Christoph Kraemer, Christian Israel Lackner, and Christian Kiefer.

Phoebe, a Negro child belonging to the widow Bohrmann, born in Aug., 1774, baptized Jan. 4, 1774. Sponsors: Maria Magdalena Bohrmann and Joh. Fried. Lackner.

Christopher, Son of Christopher Hudson, born on the 10th of Sept., 1774, baptized on the 31st of Jan., 1775. Godfathers both Parents and Robert Hudson. (in English)

Hanna, daughter of Johannes Scheeraus and his wife Maria Magdalena, was born Feb. 5, 1775, baptized the same day. Sponsors: John Michel and his wife Maria.

Hanna Elisabeth, daughter of Mr. [left unfilled] Schrind from Pennsylvania, was born Dec. 26, 1774, and baptized March 2, 1775. Sponsors were Mr. [left unfilled] Kuebler and Hannah his wife from Goshen.

Johann Caspar, son of Mr. Johann Caspar Kreiner in Halifax, was born in July, 1774, and received lay baptism in the month of Aug., 1774, which was confirmed March 16, 1775. Sponsors were Mr. Joh. Caspar Kreiner and Louis Louis, wife of Mr. Louis.

Carolina, Daughter of John Long in Halifax, born on the 5th of Jan., 1773, baptized on the 16th of March, 1775, both Parents being Godfathers and Mr. Casp. Kreiner and Carolina Kreiner. (in English)

Jane and Rose, Children of James Miller, the First born in the Month [left unfilled], 1773, the Second in the Month of Jan., 1775, both baptized on the 11th of March, 1775, Mr. John Caspar Kreiner and Rosina Hirschman were Godfathers. (in English)

Martha, Daughter of John Johnston, born the 15th of Sept., 1773, and baptized on the 16th of March, 1775. Parents Godfather and Godmother. (in English)

John, Son of John Johnston, born in the Month of Aug., 1774, baptized on the 16th of March, 1775, both Parents being Witnesses. (in English)

David, Son of Mathew Artis in Beach Eyland, two years old, was baptized on the 24th of March, 1775, both Parents being Witnesses. (in English)

David Conrad, Son of John Conrad Nail and Rose Maria his Wife, born in the Month of Nov., 1774, baptized on the 24th of March. Godfather, Mr. John Murray and Mr. Nail. (in English)

Sarah, Daughter of John Staehle, born in the Month of April, 1774, baptized on the 24th of March, 1775. Godfather, Mr. David Zubly and the Mother. (in English)

Abigail, Daughter of Daniel Miller and Sarah his Wife, was born on the 1st Day of Aug., 1770, baptized on the 26th of March, 1775. (in English)

Catharina, daughter of Mr. Nicolaus Schubtrein and his wife Margaretha, was born April 3, 1775, and baptized the same day. Sponsors were Mr. Joseph Schubtrein and his wife.

Johanna, daughter of Johannes Scheeraus and his wife, was born April 10, 1775, and baptized on the 11th. Sponsors were Johannes Binninger and Johanna his wife.

Christoph Friedrich, son of Pastor Christoph Friedrich Triebner and Friederika Maria his wife, was born July 12, 1775, in the evening at 8 o'clock, and on the 13th committed to the Lord Christ by holy baptism. Sponsors were Mr. Johann Caspar Wertsch, Mr. Christoph Kraemer, Salome Lemcke and Timotheus Lemcke.

Solomo, son of Johannes Maurer and his wife Maria Magdalena, was born Oct. 7, 1775, and baptized Oct. 8, 1775. Sponsors were Salomo Zant and Dorothea his wife and Johannes Floerl.

Maria, daughter of Matthias Biddenbach and Anna his wife, was born Oct. 10, 1775 in the night, and baptized on the 11th. Sponsors were Mr. Christoph Kraemer and Catharina his wife and Mrs. Friederika Maria Triebner.

Josua Peter, son of Johann Peter Freyermuth and his wife Catharina, was born Oct. 18, 1775, and baptized on the 19th. Sponsors were Christoph Fried. Triebner, Anna Eva Haberer, Daniel Weitmann, and Anna Margareth Groll.

William, Son of William King and Sarah his wife, being born on the 10th Day of April, 1775, and baptized on the eight of Aug., 1775, both Parents stood Godfather and Godmother. (in English)

James Little, Son of James Goldwire and his wife, being born in the 25th Day of May, 1775, and baptized on the 25th of Oct., 1775, both Parents being Godfathers. (in English)

Elisabeth, Daughter of John Caspar Hirschman and his Wife at Halifax, being born on the 27th Day of May, 1775, and christened on the 1st of Dec. Jacob Ihle. (in English)

Mary Newman, Spouse of John Kittle living in Carolina, was baptized on the Seventh Day of Nov., 1775 just before they were married in the Presence of the Company, who accompanied them. (in English)

1776

James Jennereth, Son of Henry Jennereth and Elisabeth his Wife, was born on the tenth Day of Dec., 1775, baptized on the 16th of Feb., 1776. Godfathers Charles de Trushit and Peter Ganrer instead of Mr. Hartstone. (in English)

John Louis, Son of Carter Crawfort and Mary his Wife, was born on the 20th of Feb., 1776, baptized on the 10th of April, 1776. Godfather were John Louis Venieur and Christiana Hammerer from Burrysburry. (in English)

John Reignier Kettle, Son of Peter Kettle and his Wifes Elizabeth, was born on the 26th of May, 1775, baptized on the 2d Day of May, 1776. Godfather both Parents. (in English)

Jacob, Son of Peter Kettle and Elisabeth his Wifes, being born on the 15th of Dec., 1775, baptized on the 2d of May, 1776. Godfathers both Parents. (in English)

Johann Georg, son of Johannes Lastinger and his wife Barbara, was born Nov. 24, 1776, baptized Sept. 12, 1776. Sponsors were Johann Georg Mengersdorff and Magdalena Gruber.

David, a Negro child belonging to the estate of the deceased Urban Bunz, was born Sept. [left unfilled], 1776, and baptized Oct. [left unfilled], 1776. Sponsors were Anna Margaretha Bunz, Anna Barbara Bunz, and Christopher Bunz.

Mary, Daughter of William Stafford and Mary Anne his Wife, being born the 22d of May, 1774, baptized on the 5th Day of Oct., 1776. Godfather both Parents. (in English)

Abraham, Son of William Stafford and Mary Anne his Wife, being born on 7th Day of Sept., 1776, and baptized on the 5th of Oct., 1776. Godfathers both Parents. (in English)

John Grumbling, Son of Valendine and Elizabeth his Wife, was born on the 1st Day of Nov., 1773, baptized on the 30th Day of Oct., 1776. Godfather Johann Philip Paulitsch and Anna Magdalene Paulitsch. (in English)

Elisabeth, Daughter of Valendine Grumbling and Elisabeth his wife, was born on the 31st of Aug. 1775, baptized on the 30th of Oct. 1776. Godfathers Johann Philip Paulitsch and Anne Magdalena Paulitsch. (in English)

Margaretha, Daughter of Andrew Bird and Elizabeth his Wifes, being born the first of Aug., 1776, baptized on the 29th of Dec., 1776. Godfathers Freedrick Rester and Mary Magdalen his Wife. (in English)

Susannah, a Negro girl belonging to Christina Kiefer, was born [left unfilled], 1776, and baptized [left unfilled]. Sponsors were Christina Kiefer and widow Dorothea Floerl.

Salome, a Negro girl belonging to the estate of Urban Bunz, was born March 10, 1776, and baptized April 12th. Sponsors were Widow Bunz and Anna Barbara Bunz.

1777

Georg Dresler, Son of Georg Dresler, born on the 7th of March, 1777, baptized on the 13th of March, 1777. Godfathers Mr. Georg Ducker, John Lohrman and Henriette Ducker. (in English)

Johann Michael, son of Michael Mak and his wife, was born Oct. [left unfilled], 1776 and baptized the next day. Sponsors were Johannes Oechsle and Elisabeth his wife.

Timotheus, son of Andreas Gnan and his wife Anna Franziska, was born Dec. 2, 1775, and baptized the following day. Sponsors were Mr. Timotheus Lemcke, Salome Lemcke and Daniel Weitman.

Abraham, Son of Nicolaus Strohbard and Mary Anne his Wifes, being born on the fift of April, 1777, baptized on the 29th of April, 1777, Godfathers being Abraham Mengersdorff and Mary Mengersdorff his Wife. (in English)

Anne, Daughter of John Strohbard and Anne his Wifes, born on the 12th of Feb., 1777, baptized on the 29th of April, 1777, Godfathers being Jacob Strohbard and Judith his Wife and Catharina Inoi and Gideon Kirk. (in English)

Johannes and Catharina, twins of Israel Leimberger and Apelone his wife, were born April 26, 1777, baptized the 27th. Sponsors were Samuel Krauss and Judith his wife, Georg Ducker and his wife from Goshen.

Martha, Daughter of John Wilson and Susannah his Wifes being born the 29th of April 1777 baptized on the 27th of May, 1777. Godfather John Wilson and Martha Bishop. (in English)

Mary, Daughter of John Stephen and Elisabeth Dresler, being born on the End of April, 1777, baptized on the 9th of May 1777. Godf. and Mother Elisabeth Griffin and William Milbrook. (in English)

William Francis, Son of James Port and Catharina Mukenfuss, being born on the 14th of Dec., 1776, baptized on the 24th of June, 1777. Godfathers, Mr. William Wylley instead Richard Wylles and the Father James Port. (in English)

Georg Dresler, Son of Georg Dresler, born on the 7th of March, 1777, baptized on the 13th, 1777. Godfathers, Mr. Georg

Ducker and John Lohrman and Henrietta Ducker. (in English) (this item stricken out because repeated)

Sarah, Daughter of John Penrose and Martha, being born on the 14th Day of Nov., 1776, baptized on the 8th of July, 1777. Godfather, Godhilf Shmidt, Mary Mag., Christiana Nies. (in English)

Magdelena, daughter of Johannes Scherraus and his wife Maria Magdalena, was born the [left unfilled], 1777, and baptized the next day. Sponsors were Johannes Michel and Maria his wife.

Salome, daughter of Joh. Christoph Kraemer and his wife Anna Catharina, was born May 14, 1777, and baptized the 15th. Sponsors were Christoph Friedrich Triebner and his wife Mrs. Maria Friederika, Mr. Johann Hangleiter, and Maria Magdalena his wife.

Elisabeth, daughter of Joh. Caspar Wertsch and Elisabeth his wife, was born Aug. 15, 1777, and baptized on the 16th. Sponsors: Johann Caspar Wertsch and wife, Friederika Maria Triebner.

Salome, daughter of Ludewich Ernst and his wife Christina, was born Sept. 8, 1777, and baptized Sept. 13th. Sponsors: Samuel Kraus and Judith his wife, Joh. Zipperer and his wife.

Caspar William, Son of Francis Vauchier and his Wifes being born on the 25th Day of Sept., 1777, and baptized on the 19th Ditto. Godfathers being John Caspar Muets and Dorothea Lachner. (in English)

Obedience, Daughter of John Jones and Susannah his Wifes, being born on the 13th of Aug., 1773, baptized on the 9th of Oct., 1777. Godfathers both Parents. (in English)

William, Son of John Jones and Susannah his Wifes, being born on the fourtheenth of June, 1777, baptized on the 9th of Octbr., 1777. (in English)

Nancy, Daughter of John Kettle and Polly his Wifes, being born the 13th of Feb., 1777, baptized on the 9th of Oct., 1777. Godfathers both Parents. (in English)

Christian, son of Joh. Hangleiter and Maria Magdalena his wife, was born Oct. 10, 1777, and baptized the next day. Sponsors were Mr. Christoph Kraemer and his wife Catharina.

David, Son of Henrich Christoph Burgermeister, born on the 30th Day of Sept., 1777, baptized on the 13th of Oct., 1777. Godfathers, Jacob Mengersdorff and Christiana his Wife. (in English)

John, Son of Jacob Mengersdorff and Christiana Elisabeth his Wifes, being born the 10th of Sept., 1777, baptized the 13th of Oct., 1777. Godfather, Henrich Christoph Burgermeister and Margaretha his Wife. (in English)

Wilhelm, son of Mr. Joh. Friedrich Schrimpf and his wife Christiana Elisabeth, born Oct. 14, 1777, and baptized the 20th. Sponsors were Christian Steiner and Gratiosa Schweiger.

Jane Plyth, born the 25th of May, 1775, and James Plyth, born on the 15th of June, 1777, children of John Plyth, being christened on the 5th of Nov., 1777. Godfathers both Parents. (in English)

Salomo, son of Johann Georg Zittrauer and Maria his wife, was born Nov. 14, 1777, and baptized Nov. 28, 1777.

Elisabeth, daughter of David Steiner and Anna Margaretha his wife, was born Dec. 6, 1777, and baptized on the 8th. Sponsors were Samuel Kraus and Judith his wife and Margareth Schweiger.

Henry, Son of Wells and Elisabeth his Wifes, being born on the 14th of Aug., 1774, baptized on the 12th of Nov., 1777. Godfathers being both Parents. (in English)

Samuel, Son of Samuel Wilkons, born on the 4th of March, 1776, baptized on the 12th of Nov., 1777. (in English)

Elizabeth, two years, and David two years and three Months, Children of Nathan Davis and Mary his wife, being bapt. on the 12th Day of Nov., 1777. (in English)

Georg Henry, four years, and Elisabeth two years and three Months old Children of Martin Sheidman, being baptiz. on the 12th of Nov., 1777. (in English)

Sarah, Daughter of Mr. Cambell and Sarah his Wife, being born on the 30th of Sept., 1773, bapt. on the 12th of Nov., 1777. (in English)

The following Six Children of Mrs. Allen a Widow living at the Blak Swamp having been bapt. on the 12th of Nov., 1777. 1.) Jonathan, born the 16th of Nov., 1761. 2.) Sarah, born on the 26th of March, 1764. 3.) William, born on the 2 of July, 1768. 4.) Mary, born on the 24th of Sept., 1770. 5.) Catharine, born on the 20th of Jan., 1773. 6.) Elisabeth. (in English)

Elisabeth, Daughter of Louis Margon, being born on the 10th of Jan., 1777. (in English)

Mattheus, son of Mattheus Biddenbach and his wife Anna, was born Dec. 28, 1777, and baptized on the 29th. Sponsors were Christoph Friedrich Triebner and his wife Maria, and Mr. Christoph Kraemer and Catharina his wife.

1778

Timotheus Traugott, son of Christoph Friedrich Triebner and his wife Friederika Maria, was born Dec. 29, 1777, and baptized Jan. 1, 1778. Sponsors were Mr. Christoph Kraemer and Mrs. Elisabeth Wertsch, Mr. Daniel Weitmann and his wife Salome.

Salome, daughter of Salomo Schrempf and his wife Christiana Elisabeth, was born Jan. 28, 1778, and baptized on the

19th. Sponsors: Andreas Sekinger and Catharina his wife and Judith Kraus.

Johanna Juliana, daughter of Mr. Jacob Buehler and his wife Christiana Elisabeth, was born in the night between Feb. 10 and 11, 1778, and baptized on the 13th. Sponsors were Johannes Mezger, Catharina Michler, Mrs. Elisabeth Wertsch, and Catharina Gravenstein.

Samuel, Son of Christopher Hudson and Sarah his wifes, being born on June 26th, 1777, and baptized the 12th of Feb., 1778. Godfathers being both Parents. (in English)

John, Son of Thomas Garneth and Rachel his Wife, being born on the 4th of Dec., 1776, bapt. on the 12th of Feb., 1778. Godfather being both Parents. (in English)

Jeremias, son of Mr. Johann Kuebler and Elisabeth his wife, was born March 16, 1778, and baptized on the 19th. Sponsors were Mr. [left unfilled] Frisch and his wife Susannah and Johann Philip Schneider and his wife.

Elisabeth, daughter of Johann Remshardt and Christiana Elisabeth his wife, was born March 22, 1778, and baptized on the 24th. Sponsors are Samuel Kraus and Judith his wife and Johanna Lackner.

Christian, son of Joh. Eigel and his wife, was born March 28, 1778, and baptized on the 30th. Sponsors were Christian Zipperer and his wife and Ludwig Frisch and his wife.

Salomo, son of Johannes Maurer and his wife Anna, was born April 11, 1778, and baptized on the 12th. Mr. Christoph Kraemer and Catharina his wife were sponsors.

Lydia, daughter of Jacob Kiefer and his wife Dorothea, was born April 13, 1778, and baptized onthe 18th. Mr. Kuebler and his wife were sponsors.

Andreas, son of Johannes Lastinger and his wife, and Elisabeth, a pair of twins, were born Feb. 12, 1778, and baptized April 24, 1778. Sponsors were Georg Mengersdorff and Gotthilf Israel Schmidt, Maria Magdalena Gruber and Christiana Niess.

Hanna, daughter of Jacob Heussler and Anna Maria his wife, was born June 12, 1778, and baptized on the 17th. Sponsors are Ernst Christian Zittrauer and Johanna his wife.

Elisabeth, daughter of Israel Rieser and his wife Hanna, was born July 23, 1778, and baptized the next day. Sponsors were Nathanael Rieser and Dorothea his wife besides Dorothea Zant, widow.

James, Son of William King, being old [left unfillled], has been baptized Aug. 6th, 1778, Godfather being the Childs Father and Mother Elizabeth Wertsch. (in English)

Friedrich Wilhelm Iliner, a soldier's son of Col. Wight's battalion, was born Aug. 9, 1778, and baptized on the 12th. Sponsors were Georg Unselt and Miss Cath. Hekel in Savannah. (in English)

David, son of John Helmle and his wife Maria Magd., was born Aug. 17, 1778, and baptized Aug. 21st. Sponsors: Christian Steiner and his wife, D. Maxen and his wife of Goshen.

Christiana, daughter of Andreas Sekinger and his wife Catharina, was born Aug. 23, 1778, and baptized the next day. Sponsors were Christian Israel Leimberger, the Widow Flerl, and Georg Ziegler and his wife.

Johanna Salome, daughter of the schoolmaster Daniel Weitmann and Salome his wife, was born Aug. 31, 1778, and baptized on Sept. 2nd. Sponsors: Christoph Friedrich Triebner and Friederika Maria his wife and Johanna Christiana Lemcke.

Andreas, son of Andreas Gnan and his wife Anna Franziska, was born Sept. 3, 1778, and baptized on the 4th. Sponsors:

Daniel Weitmann and Salome his wife, who were represented by Johanna Christiana Lemcke, and Johann Rothenberger.

Salome, daughter of Georg Gruber, was born Nov. 1, 1778, and baptized on the 2nd. Sponsors: Jacob Gnan and Hanna his wife and Catharine Gravenstein.

Margaret, daughter of Jacob Gnan and his wife Hanna, was born Nov. 26, 1778, and baptized the same day. Sponsors were Johann Georg Gruber and his wife and Joh. Paulus and his wife.

Maria, a soldier's child, which Mr. Jacob Buehler adopted, was baptized on Nov. 8, 1778. Mr. Jacob Buehler and his wife were sponsors.

Sophia, a Negro child belong to Christina Kiefer, was born Nov. 20, and baptized Nov. 21, 1778. Christina Kiefer and Dorothea Flerl were sponsors.

Gratiosa, daughter of Ernst Zittrauer and his wife Johanna, was born Dec. 21, 1778, and baptized on the 22nd. Sponsors were Jonathan Zipperer, who was represented by Simon Reiter, and Gratiosa Zipperer.

1779

Maria, daughter of Benjamin Rieser and Catharina his wife, was born Jan. 13, 1779, and baptized the next day. Sponsors were Margaretha Hek and Georg Bechtle.

Johann Christoph, son of Johann Christoph Bunz and his wife, was born Jan. 26, 1779, and baptized the next day. Sponsors: Christoph Kraemer and Catharina his wife, Joh. Hangleiter and his wife.

Jonathan Christian, son of Jonathan Zipperer and Gratiosa his wife, was born Jan. 25, 1779, and baptized the next day.

[left unfilled], daughter of Benjamin Glaner and his wife, was born Feb. 4, 1779, and baptized on the 8th. Sponsors were Joh. Adam Nessler and Dorothea his wife.

Hanna, daughter of Joh. Rudolph Binninger and his wife Johanna, was born Feb. 10, 1779, and baptized on the 11th. Sponsors: Jacob Meier and Hanna Juliana his wife.

Elisabeth Schmidt, daughter of Jerem. Tonnewan and his wife Sarah, six months old, was baptized March 5, 1779. Sponsors both parents. (mixed language)

Sarah Evel. Quin, Daughter of Georg Quin and Francis his Wife, being born on the 2d day of Jan., 1778, baptized on the 15th of March, 1779. Godfathers, Samuel Ihle, Susannah Moore. (in English)

Salome, Daughter of John Caspar Hirshman and Rosina his Wife, being born on the 16th of Jan., 1779, baptized 15th March, 1779. Sponsors: John Heusler and his Wife, Philip Sheides and his Wife and Elisabeth Kuebler. (in English)

Hanna, daughter of Nikolaus Schubtrein and his wife Margaretha, was born April 13, 1779, baptized the 14th, 1779. Sponsors were Mr. Joseph Schubtrein and Agnesia Schubtrein.

James, Son of John Lohrman and his Wife, being born the 5th of April, 1779, baptized the 12th of April, 1779. Godfathers and Godm., John Kuebler and his Wife. (in English)

Christian, son of Dr. Lang and his wife Maria Magdalena, was born May 11, 1779, about 4 o'clock in the morning. Sponsors were Mr. Christian Scheerer, who was represented by Joh. Christoph Stroebel.

Anna Maria, daughter of Mr. Joh. Frisch and his wife Susanna, was born April 30, 1779, and baptized May 6, 1779. Sponsors were David Steiner and Anna Margareth his wife.

Samuel, son of Christian Steiner and Dorothea his wife, was born May 17, 1779, and baptized the next day. Sponsors: Joseph Schubtrein and Agnesia his wife.

Lydia, daughter of Georg Ziegler and his wife Catharina, was born may 18, 1779, and baptized the next day. Sponsors were David Steiner and Hanna Margaretha his wife.

Gotthilf Israel, son of Leonhardt Niess and his wife Christiana, was born May 18, 1779, and baptized May 22, 1779. Sponsors, Gotthilf Israel Schmidt and Hannah Elisabeth his wife and Mr. Jacob Meier.

Margaretha, daughter of Jacob Kraus and Susanna his wife, was born April 2, 1779, and baptized on June 10th. Both parents were sponsors.

Israel, son of Johannes Heinle and his wife Barbara, was born July 14, 1779, and baptized Aug. 8, 1779. Sponsors were Israel Kieffer, David Steiner, who was represented by Joh. Renz, and Anna Margaretha Steiner.

Anna, daughter of Lucas Ziegler and his wife Anna, was born June 26, 1779, and baptized the next day. Sponsors: Joh. Casp. Waldhauer, who was represented by Georg Gnan, and Margaretha Waldhauer and Mrs. Rebeka Dieter.

Christina, daughter of Nathanael Rieser and Dorothea, his wife, was born July 7, 1779, and baptized on the 10th. Sponsors: Israel Rieser and his wife, Gotthilf Israel Schmidt and Hannah Elis. his wife.

Salome, the illegitimate daughter of Johann Martin Daescher and Maria Friederika Scheeraus, was born May 23, 1779, and baptized Sept. 2, 1779. Sponsors: Mr. Christoph Kraemer and Catharine Kraemer and Jonathan Fezir (Fetzer) and his wife Anna Magdalena.

Dorothea, daughter of Joh. Scheeraus, was born May 16, 1779, and baptized on the [left unfilled]. Joh. Rudolph Binninger and his wife Johanna were sponsors.

Salomo, son of Joh. Glaner and his wife, was born Aug. 31, 1779, baptized on Sept. 1st. Sponsors were Johann Adam Nesseler and Dorothea his wife and Johannes Maurer, who was represented by Andreas Sekinger and Anna his wife.

Dina, daughter of William Stafford and Anna Mary Stafford, resident in Carolina, was born March 15, 1778, and baptized Sept. 2, 1779. Sponsors were Mr. Jacob Meier and Anna Juliana Meier.

1780

David, son of Ludwich Ernst and his wife, was born Jan. [left unfilled], 1780, baptized Feb. 27th. Sponsors were Jonathan Zipperer and his wife and Elisabeth Kiebler.

Salomo, son of Peter Freymuth and Catharina his wife, was born Feb. 25, 1780, and baptized on the 28th. Sponsors were Pastor Triebner and his wife Maria Friederika, Daniel Weitman, and widow Anna Eva Habor.

Sarah Connell, Daughter of Thomas Connell in Washington County in Maryland, was born on the 28th Day of June, 1778, baptized on the 27th Day of Jan., 1780. Godfhar. and Godmother are Christopher Buntz, Anne Barbara Buntz and Rosina Miller together with the Mother of the Child Mary Connell. (in English)

Mary, Daughter of Richard Stephen and Anne his Wifes, has been born the 15th of May, 1776, and baptized the 27th of June, 1780. Parents being Godfathers. (in English)

Anne, Daughter of Richard Stephen and Anne his Wifes, has been born the 16th of April, 1778, baptized the 27th of June, 1780. Parents being Godfathers. (in English)

Elisabeth, daughter of Joh. Adam Nessler and Dorothea his wife, was born Nov. [left unfilled], 1779, and baptized July 22, 1780. Sponsors were Dorothea Floerl and Christina Kiefer and Ernst Zittrauer.

Catharina, daughter of Johannes Scheeraus in Bethany, was born Sept. 9, 1780, and baptized on the 10th. Sponsors are Johannes Michel and Maria his wife, who was represented by her daughter Catharina Rieser.

Sarah, Daughter of Nathaniel Miller and his Wifes, has been born the 28th Day of Nov., 1778, baptized the 15th Day of Sept. 1780. Godfather, Robin Williamson and Sarah Miller Mother of the Child. (in English)

Mary, Daughter of John Lastinger and Anne Barbara his Wifes, being born the 22d of May, 1780, baptized the 29th of Sept., 1780. Samuel Kraus and his Wife Judith being Godfather and Godmother. (in English)

William, Son of John Gruber and Magdalen his Wifes, being born the 13th of Dec., 1778, baptized the 29th of Sept., 1780. Godfather and Godmother, Samuel Kraus and Judith his Wife. (in English)

Johann Jacob, son of Johann Jacob Jaekle and Anna Regina his wife, was born Nov. 18, 1780, and baptized on the 21st. Sponsors were John Caspar Muek and Catharina his wife.

David Posthumus, son of the deceased Christian Israel Leimberger and his wife Apelona, was born Nov. 28th, and baptized on the 29th. Sponsors: Samuel Kraus and Judith his wife.

Mary, Daughter of Samuel Ihle and his Wife, being born on the 6th Day of March, 1780, baptized the 19th of Nov., 1780. Godfathers, Christian Zipperer, Sarah Moor, and Nancy Moore. (in English)

1781

Georg, Son of Jacob Mengersdorff and Christiana his Wifes, being born the 15th of Octobr., 1780, baptized on the 12th of Jan., 1781. Godfathers, Thomas Geiger and Mary his Wife. (in English)

Juliana Christiana, daughter of Jacob Buehler and his wife, was born Feb. 10, 1781 in the night, and baptized on the 11th. Sponsors were Jacob Mezger and Salome his wife and Johanna Christiana Lemcke.

Samuel Radliff, Son of Elisa Radliff and Mary, born the 15th of Sept., 1779, baptized the 22d of Feb., 1781. Godfathers being both Parents. (in English)

Elisabeth, Daughter of Elisa Radliff and Elisabeth his Wifes, born the 4th of Nov., 1781. Godfathers were both Parents. (in English)

Matthaeus, son of Matthaeus Weinkauf and his wife, was born Sept. [left unfilled], 1781, and baptized Sept. 26th. Sponsors were Johann Heusler, Matthias Muek, and his wife.

Maria Magdalena, daughter of Johannes Heussler and his wife, was born Sept. [left unfilled], 1781, and baptized on the 26th. Sponsors were Mattheus Weinkauf and Joh. Caspar Muek and his wife.

Salome, daughter of Andrew Gnan and his wife Anna Franciska, was born Sept. 27th, and baptized on the 29th. Sponsors were Johanna Lemcke and Daniel Weitman and his wife.

On the 29th of Sept., 1781, a stillborn daughter was born to me by my wife Friederica Maria Triebner.

Christina, daughter of Johannes Glaner and his wife Hanna Elisabeth, was born Sept. 26, 1781, and baptized on the 30th. Sponsors were Mr. Christoph Kraemer and his wife Catharina.

Christoph (?), son of Mr. Christoph Kraemer, was born Sept. 15th early about one o'clock, and baptized the same day. Sponsors were Christoph Friedrich Triebner and Mrs. Friederica Maria his wife, Mr. Joh. Hangleiter and Maria Magdalena his wife.

Catharina, Mr. Joh. Hangleiter's Negro child, was born Oct. 5, 1781, and baptized on the 15th. Witnesses: Joh. Hangleiter and his wife.

Maria, daughter of Jacob Ihle and his wife Hanna, was born Oct. [left unfilled], 1781, and baptized on Nov. 1st. Sponsors were Johannes Ihle and Catharina his wife and Caspar Muek and his wife.

Sarah, Daughter of Adam Morisson and Elisabeth his Wifes, was born the 16 of Octobr., 1781, and baptized the 19th of Nov., 1781. Godfathers, the Mother and David McGoun and Elisabeth Steward. (in English)

Names and Circumstances of all the People Married Here Since February 1754

1754

Christian Desher and Anna Christina Mayer were joined in marriage Feb. 19, 1754. An address was delivered on Psalms 119:105.

Joh. Georg Haid and Eleanora Kurtz entered into holy matrimony with each other March 4, 1754. Hebrews 2:18.

Johann Martin Paulitsch and Ursula Schweighofer were united in marriage April 22, 1754. Their wedding verse was John 15:14.

On the same day also

Georg Rieser and the widow Anna Dorothea Mayer entered into holy matrimony with each other.

Johann Caspar Beth and Eva Maria Zegler were joined in marriage the first Tuesday after Whitsunday, 1754. He lives in Goshen.

Johann Rentz and Barbara Unselt were joined in marriage Nov. 26, 1754. The text was Ephesians 4:23, 24.

Georg Michael Weber and Maria Magdalena Greiner were joined in marriage the same day.

1755

Wolfgang Mackh and the widow Anna Barbara Mayerhoefer of Purrysburg were united in marriage Feb. 24, 1755.

Johannes Paulus of the 3rd Swabian Transport was united in marriage with the widow Maria Ursula Groll, April 1, 1755.

Johann Georg Niess and Maria Oexle were joined in marriage June 24, 1755.

Bartholomeus Mackh and Maria Staud were united in marriage July 1, 1755. The text was I Peter 3:9.

Caspar Klock of Purrysburg and the widow Barbara Schaeffer were united in marriage July 28, 1755.

Jacob Hueter and the widow Anna Gerber were joined in marriage Nov. 19, 1755.

Jacob Frick and Anna Catharina Strubler of Purrysburg were united in marriage here Nov. 24, 1755.

Johannes Klein and Maria Christina Oechsle were joined in marriage Nov. 25, 1755.

Georg Friedrich Rester from Durlach and Maria Margaretha Mengersdorf were joined in marriage Dec. 7, 1755.

1756

Andreas Seckinger and the widow Agnes Ziegler were joined in marriage May 17, 1756. The text was from John 16:22.

On May 31, 1756, Johann Georg Mueller and the widow Rosina Schubdrein were joined in marriage. Psalms 94:19.

Johann Georg Ziegler and Anna Catherina Rau were joined in marriage June 1, 1756.

Johann Conrad Frickinger and Barbara Greuser were united in marriage June 8, 1756. The text was Psalms 143:10.

Andreas Greiner and Barbara Hirschmann were joined in marriage July 26, 1756.

Mathias von Alman and Anna Magdalena Folcker were united in marriage here Aug. 6, 1756.

Jacob Friedrich Kiefer was united in marriage with a young woman from Carolina, Anna Maria Winnagler, Aug. 3, 1756. The text was Sirach. 50:24-26.

Jacob Tussing was united in marriage with the widow Maria Kaemmel, Sept. 14, 1756. Text Matthew 24:37-39.

Hugh Kennedy was united in marriage with the widow Schrempf, Sept. 22.

N. B. — Up to this point those married were sent on Dec. 6, 1756 to Mr. Broughton.

1757

Conrad Eckart of Frankfurt was joined in marriage with the widow Anna Maria Hueber, Jan. 4, 1757. Text, Luke 11:28.

Nehemiah Dindal was united in marriage with Elisabeth Miller of Halifax, Jan. 3, 1757.

Thomas Walker of Briar Creek was united in marriage in the presence of witnesses with an unmarried woman of Briar Creek by the name Rebecca Emmanuel, Jan. 27, 1757.

Michael Dauner and the widow Waldpurga Oechsle were joined in marriage March 22, 1757.

Jacob Kuhn, a German from Charlestown of Lutheran confession, was united in marriage with Barbara Bandle, a Reformed widow from Purrysburg, June 27, 1757.

Hans Pfluger and Barbara Rau were joined in marriage, Aug. 24, 1757.

Sebastian Hasenlauer and Elisabeth Honold, née Rau, were joined in marriage Oct. 12, 1757.

1758

James Fletcher and Margaret Pigg were joined in marriage Feb. 6, 1758 in Halifax.

Johann Caspar Greiner was united in marriage with the widow Caroline Magdalene Bornemann, Feb. 7, 1758 in Halifax.

Jacob Mohr, from Goshen, was united in marriage with the widow Elisabeth Walliser, here in Ebenezer, March 2, 1758.

Johann Caspar Wertsch and Miss Hanna Elisabeth Gronau were united in marriage March 14, 1758. The wedding sermon consisted of inculcating beautiful passages, which treat of the good that believers in Christ have and enjoy here in their discipleship of the cross, as in Wisdom 3:9; Sirach 34:14-20; Isaiah 45:24; I Corinthians 1:30, from which may the Lord grant to them and all who heard them an abiding blessing.

Johann Georg Schneider and Anna Barbara Schneider were joined in marriage March 21, 1758.

James Ducker and Alice Heaton were joined in marriage April 15, 1758.

Joh. Schneider and Catherina Grimminger were joined in marriage June 7, 1758.

Jacob Caspar Waldhauer and Agnesia Ziegler were joined in marriage June 27, 1758.

Nicolaus Schubdrein and Anna Maria Zuercher were joined in marriage July 4 of the same year.

Thomas Schweighofer and Hanna Flerl were joined in marriage Aug. 1, 1758.

Thomas Davis of Mount Pleasant and the widow Jane Southerland were joined in marriage Aug 17, 1758.

1758

Samuel Greves and Margareth Huber were joined in marriage Nov. 7, 1758.

Georg Gruber and Elisabeth Schwartzwaelder were joined in marriage Nov. 14, 1758.

Johann Michael Zischler was united in marriage with the widow Barbara Lackner, née Haeusler, Nov. 21, 1758 in the church in Goshen.

Johann Martin Rheinlaender and Maria Kalcher were united in marriage Dec. 12, 1758.

Johann Jacob Heuseler and Anna Maria Haefner were joined in marriage Dec. 12, 1758.

Lucas Moser was united in marriage with the widow Anna Catherina Kuebler from Goshen, Dec. 28, 1758.

1759

Jacob Gnann was united in marriage with the widow Maria Margareth Depp, Jan. 23, 1759.

Johann Scherraus and Anna Maria Mohr were joined in marriage Feb. 20, 1759 in Goshen.

Samuel Royall and Esther Williams were united in marriage here May 8, 1759.

Francis Pugh and Martha Raines were united in marriage Feb. 12, 1759.

John Hopkins and Sarah Thomas were united in marriage March 21, 1759.

Gregorius Stierle, from Purrysburg, was united in marriage here with Maria Rosina Hammer, May 16, 1759.

Johann Lohrmann and Susanna Humbart were united in marriage May 28, 1759.

Johann Christoph Heintz and Regina Barbara Hirsch were united in marriage Aug. 15, 1759.

1760

Gabriel Maurer and Anna Eigel were united in marriage Feb. 13, 1760.

Johannes Heinle and Maria Kogler were joined in marriage Feb. 19, 1760. Galatians 6:15, 16.

Caspar Gerber, a cabinet maker from Savannah, a widower, was united in marriage with Christina Barbara Haefner, the third daughter of the widow Straub, May 20, 1760. Isaiah 44:3, 4.

Georg Fischer was united in marriage with the widow Anna Dorothea Rieser, June 24, 1760.

John Wilson, an Englishman, was united in marriage with Maria Riedelsperger, Nov. 19, 1760.

Up to this point those married reported to London.

Christian Steiner and Dorothea Farr were united in marriage Dec. 16, 1760. Psalms 37:37.

1761

Martin Fettler of Savannah and Anna Ursula Moser were united in marriage Feb. 3, 1761.

Georg Schweiger and the widow Margareta Zittrauer were united in marriage May 19, 1761.

Joh. Georg Zittrauer was on the same day, May 19, 1761, united in marriage with Catharina Brandwein.

Joh. Georg Niess was united in marriage with the widow Sibyll Regina Geiger, Sept. 1, 1761. The wedding verse was Psalms 55: "Cast thy burden upon the Lord."

1762

In 1762 there were no marriages.

1763

David Steiner was joined in marriage with Anna Margaret Zimmerebener, Feb. 1, 1763.

Johann Justus Gravenstein and Catharina Bidenbach were united in marriage Feb. 22, 1763.

Johann Martin Greiner was united in marriage with Maria Eischperger, May 24, 1763.

Johann Martin Rheinlaender was united in marriage with Friedericka Catharina Bruckner, May 31, 1763.

Georg Schleich and Maria Magdalena Maurer were united in marriage Aug. 21, 1763.

N. B. — Up to this point the marriages have been reported.

1764

Samuel Kraus and Judith Flerl were united in marriage Jan. 24, 1764, in Zion Church.

Johann Jacob Kuebler and Elisabeth Reuter were united in marriage Jan. 31, 1764.

Johann Caspar Hirschmann was on the same day, namely Jan. 31, 1764, joined in marriage with Rosina Kuebler.

Johannes Remshardt and Anna Margaretha Mueller were united in marriage Feb. 14, 1764. The wedding sermon was on I Corinthians 7:28-31.

Georg Fischer was united in marriage with Maria Mackh, May 29, 1764 in Bethany. Psalms 128:1, 2.

Sebastian Fetzer was united in marriage with the widow Anna Maria Staehli, June 12, 1764.

Peter Janson was united in marriage with Margar. Leimberger, July 31, 1764.

Christian Israel Leimberger and Apollonia Dauner were united in marriage Aug. 28, 1764.

Jacob Jaeckel from Goshen and Anna Regina Birckholter were joined in marriage in the Zion Church, Oct. 16, 1764.

N. B. — Up to this point the marriages have been reported to the Society in London.

1765

Johannes Flerl and Hanna Elisabeth Brandner were joined in marriage Jan. 15, 1765.

Johann Ulrich Fetzer and Johanna Mohr were united in marriage in Jerusalem Church, March 19, 1765.

Thomas Mackh and Maria Weinkauff were united in marriage April 16, 1765.

Johann Nikolaus Strobart from Purrysburg and Eva Maria Mengersdorff were joined in marriage in Jerusalem Church, May 7, 1765.

Johann Gruber and Maria Magdalena Kalcher were joined in marriage in Zions Church, June 4, 1765.

Lucas Ziegler and Salome Zettler were joined in marriage June 25, 1765.

Lambeth Leen and Elisabeth Catharine Zettler were joined in marriage June 25, 1765.

Leonhardt Friedrich Ebinger and Magdalena Pollinger were united in marriage June 25, 1765.

Johann Martin Burgermeister of Purrysburg, and Maria Elisabeth Mengersdorff were united in marriage in Jerusalem Church, Aug. 13, 1765.

N. B. — The marriages have been reported up to this point.

1766

Patrick Onyl (O'Neal) and Maria Krumbl were joined in marriage June 17, 1766.

Johann Adam Freyermuth and Maria Elisabeth Buehler were united in marriage Oct. 7, 1766.

Johannes Oechsle and Elisabeth Gress were joined in marriage Dec. 16, 1766.

Johannes Meyer and Christina Remshardt were joined in marriage Dec. 23, 1766. The text was Philippians 4:5, 6.

N. B. — Here begins a new number.

1767

Christian Oechsle was united in marriage with the widow Walpurg Kraeuter, Jan. 27, 1767 in Bethany. The wedding text was in Romans 12:12: "Rejoicing in hope."

Johannes Maurer and Maria Magdalena Zant were joined in marriage Feb. 24, 1767. Psalms 37: 4, 5.

Johann Jacob Kieffer and Dorothea Reuter were joined in marriage March 24, 1767, also

Salomo Zant and Elisabeth Kieffer were also united in marriage March 24, 1767. The wedding text Psalms 119:132.

Georg Ludwig Roth and Anna Fetzer were united in marriage March 31, 1767.

Johann Friederich Ochs was joined in marriage with Anna Fetzer, daughter of Sebastian Fetzer, May 19, 1767.

Johann Leonhardt Niess and Christina Elisabeth Schmied were joined in marriage May 26.

Johannes Lastinger and Anna Barbara Huber were united in marriage Sept. 29, 1767. Joshua 1:8.

Joshua Stafford and Margaret Irenmonger.

Israel Bird and Anna Stafford.

1768

Silvanus Bird and Dinah Stafford, all on Ogeechee River, were joined in marriage March 4, 1768.

John Ford and Mary More.

James Nolliboy and Catharine Gaskin, all in St. Matthews Parish, were joined in marriage March 7, 1768.

Johann Georg Rentz and Hanna Margareta Kalcher were joined in marriage March 8, 1768. John 15:14.

Matthaeus Weinkauf and Christina Mackh were joined in marriage April 12, 1768. Text, Psalms 59:16, 17.

John Stafford and Susanne Evans were lawfully married on the 26th day of May, 1768. They are living in the province of South Carolina. (in English)

John Nevil and Francis Nicson were lawfully married on the 13th day of Oct., 1768. (in English)

Salomon Perthero and Elisabeth Wiles were both lawfully married on the 25th day of Oct., 1768, in the presence of the bride's father and other people. (in English)

Johann Paul Miller and Elisabeth Maurer were joined in marriage Nov. 2, 1768.

Johann Heinle was united in marriage with the widow Maria Barbara Schneider, Nov. 22, 1768. The wedding text was Psalms 73:23, 24.

Nathan Taylor and Susannah Glazon were both lawfully married on the 8th day of Dec., 1768. (in English)

So far the number has been reported.

William Obrian and Mary Charnock were both lawfully married to each other on the 15th day of Dec., 1768. (in English)

1769

John Jeffes and Judit Dickson were both married on the 6th of Feb., 1769. (in English)

Abraham Mott and Sarah Scruggs both of St. Matthew's Parish were lawfully married on the 16th of Feb., 1769.

John Cothal Bucher and Catharine Ambar were both lawfully, according to a License, married on the Tenth of March, 1769. (in English)

Johann Friederich Briest was joined in marriage with the widow Rebecca Faul, March 28, 1769. Psalm 86:11.

John Jones and Susannah Strobart were both lawfully joined together in holy wedlock agreeable to a License this 1st day of April, 1769. (in English)

Daniel Burgsteiner and Maria Daescher were united in marriage, April 11, 1769. The wedding text was Psalms 25:10.

Mr. Christoph Friedrich Triebner and Miss Friedrika Maria Gronau were united in marriage April 18, 1769. The wedding text was Psalms 134. "May the Lord that made heaven and earth bless this couple out of Zion."

Archibald Cunningham and Rachel Robert were united in marriage April 27, 1769.

Johann Peter Freiermuth and Anna Catharine Groll were united in marriage May 23, 1769. Text: Proverbs 2:6-7.

Allen Groves and Mary Lanier were joined in marriage June 22, 1769.

John Braddock and Loucy Cook were both lawfully joined in marriage July 16, 1769.

Johann Paul Mueller, Jun. and Anna Seckinger were joined in marriage July 18, 1769. Text: Romans 7:2-4.

William Kings and Sarah Goldwire were both united in marriage here Sept. 14, 1769. (in English)

John Jones and Mary, Powel, Elias Brown, were lawfully married on the 15th of Sept., 1769. (in English)

Johann Caspar Wertsch and Elisabeth Koegler were both, after a marriage sermon on Revelations 19:5-9, united in Christian marriage Oct. 10, 1769.

John Goldwire and Elisabeth Moore were both lawfully joined in marriage here in Ebenezer, Nov. 8, 1769.

Friedrich Roesberg of Savannah was united in marriage with Johanna Cronberger Oct. 30, 1769 upon a licence received from the Governor.

John Dunn and Mary Parmer were lawfully joined in matrimony on the 28th Nov., 1769. (in English)

Jacob Heinle and the widow Christina Meyer were united in marriage in Zions Church, Dec. 12, 1769.

Up to this point the number has been reported.

1770

Johannes Scheeraus and the widow Magdalena Epinger were both legally united in Christian marriage in Bethany, Jan. 9, 1770. The wedding text, Psalms [left unfilled].

Mattheus Weinkauf and Anna Rosina Kussmaul were joined in marriage Jan. 16, 1770 in Goshen.

Friedrich Schrempf and Sarah Dixon were joined in marriage Feb. 7, 1770.

Johann Georg Heid and the widow Maria Magdalena Schleich were united in marriage Feb. 27, 1770.

Joseph Ironmonger and Sarah Johnsten were both lawfully joined in marriage March 21, 1770.

Thomas Jones and Mary Howell, after threefold preceding publication, were both lawfully joined in marriage here in Jerusalem Church, June 11, 1770.

Adam Kessler and Hannah Kiefer were joined in marriage Aug. 14, 1770.

Richard Stephens and Nancy Brady were lawfully married on the 24th of Aug., 1770.

Christian Ernest Zittrauer and Hanna Reiter were both lawfully joined in marriage Oct. 2, 1770.

Mattheus Bittenbach and Anna Paulus were both united in Christian marriage in Bethany, Nov. 7, 1770.

Thomas Campbell and Sarah Cox, both of St. Matthew's Parish, were lawfully married on the 29 of Dec., 1770. (in English)

Thomas Rolbens (Robbins?) and Sarah Harnage, both of St. Georg's Parish, have been published on three several Sundays and holy days and requiring a certificate to prove it before a Justice, 1st Jan., 1770. (in English)

1771

Robert Dickson and Suky Johns were lawfully united in marriage Jan., 1771. (in English)

Johann Michael Haberer and the widow Anna Eva Weidman were both lawfully united in Christian marriage Feb. 26, 1771. Psalms 33:18, 19, 20.

Jacob Meier and the widow Juliana Schmidt, and also Georg Gnan and Anna Franciska Rotenberger were both parties united in marriage Jan. 22, 1771. Isaiah 48:17, 18.

Michael Heinsman and Ursula Hekel were united in marriage in Zions Church, Jan. 22, 1771.

Johannes Heckel and Hanna Margaretha Heinrich were united in marriage here in Ebenezer, April 9, 1771.

James English and Mary May, both of St. Philip's Parish in Carolina, were married on the 6. of June, 1771. (in English)

Samuel Bostich and Anne Mary Mane both of St. Matthew's Parish have been married by a License from the Governor the 9 July, 1771. (in English)

Bartholomeus Neibling and Anna Maria Ochs were united in marriage in Bethany, Aug. 20, 1771.

William Blair and Sibillia Earl, both in this parish, were published three times and on Oct. 26, 1771, received a Certificate from me.

William Radlif and Diana Moon, both in St. Philip's Parish, were lawfully united in marriage here in Ebenezer, Nov. 1, 1771.

William Roger and Cilia Benson, both of this parish, were both united in marriage by me here Nov. 4, 1771.

Jonathan Cole and Nancy Radlist, both in St. Philip's Parish, were lawfully united in marriage Nov. 19, 1771.

Up to this point the number has been reported.

1772

Aaron Matthew and Mary Davey, both of St. Georg Parish have been lawfully published thrice here at Ebenezer and have desired a Certificate thereof on the 6th of Jan., 1772. (in English)

Thomas Garneth and Rachel Wissin have been married on the 8th of Jan., 1772 by a License from his Hon. the Commander. (in English)

Chaplin William and Susannah Green, both of St. Matthew's Parish, after having been lawfully published by me before the Congregation desired and received a Certificate on the 20th of Jan., 1772. (in English)

Johann Caspar Greiner and Johanna Christiana Lackner were united in marriage in Zions Church, Jan. 4, 1772.

Michael Gnan and the widow Maria Magdalena Weber were united in marriage in Ebenezer, Jan. 14, 1772.

Nikolaus Michel and Hannah Elisabeth Gugel were both united in Christian marriage Jan. 28, 1772.

John Boykin and Sarah Tanner have been lawfully married on the 20. Day of April, 1772. (in English)

Josiah Daniel and Elisabeth Dison both of Carolina, have been lawfully married on the 23 Day of April. (in English)

Abiel Perry and Sarah Asque after having been lawfully published at Ebenezer have received a Certificate thereof the 21st of July, 1772. (in English)

James Goldwire and Sarah Stewart both of St. Matthew's Parish, were both married by a License on the 18th Day of Aug., 1772. (in English)

Hardy Boykin and Susannah Young both of St. Georg's Parish, have been lawfully published before the Congregation and received a Certificate thereof on the 7th of Nov., 1772. (in English)

Johann Nicolaus Schubtrein and Margareth Haussler were both united in marriage Nov. 11, 1772.

Up to this point the number has been reported.

1773

Johann Jacob Heinle and Hanna Elisabeth Thilo were both united in Christian marriage in Zions Church, Jan. 5, 1773.

John Burnell and Winefred Wilson, both of St. Georg's Parish, were both thrice published before the Congregation, and have desired a Certificate thereof on the   of Jan., 1773. (in English)

Matthew Colson and Chloe Woods have been lawfully married Feb. 6th, 1773. (in English)

Shadrik Harper and Sarah Trager, both of Carolina, were lawfully married on the 7th of March, 1773. (in English)

Valendin Grumbley and Elisabeth Fulsher (?) were lawfully married on the 8th of March, 1773.

Peter Kettle and Elisabeth Danell were both lawfully married on the 11th of May, 1773.

William Stafford and Anne Maria Geiger of St. Philips Parish were both lawfully published on the 18th Day of May, 1773. (in English)

Charles Hall and Alley Depew were both lawfully married on the 6th Day of July, 1773.

Jacob Buehler and Christiana Elisabeth Bechtol were both united in marriage July 6th, 1773. Text: I Timothy 4:8.

Joseph Schubtrein and Agnesia Ott were both united in marriage July 6th, 1773 by Mr. R.

Johann Israel Rieser and Hanna Margaretha Schubtrein were both united in marriage in Zion, July 6, 1773.

William Milliner and Mary Goodall, both of St. Georg's Parish, were both lawfully married on the fourteenth Day of Sept., 1772. (in English)

Elijah Sadlift and Mary Stafford, both of our Parish were both lawfully married on the 23 of Nov., 1773. (in English)

Christian Preisier and Johanna Depp were both united in marriage in Zion in [left unfilled] 1773.

Jacob Gnan and Hanna Mezger were both united in Christian marriage April 6, 1773. Text: Malachi 3:14–4:12.

Johannes Remshardt and Christiana Schubtrein were both united in marriage in Zion April, 1773.

Johann Rudolph Binninger and Johanna Eger were both united in marriage Dec. 28, 1773 in Ebenezer.

1774

Benjamin Daly and Susannah Garneth were lawfully joined together in the holy Estate of Matrimony by a License on the 6th of Jan., 1774 at Mr. Garneth's House. (in English)

Jesse Busbey and Molly Pearce, both of Carolina, were both lawfully married on the 26 Day of Jan., 1774. (in English)

Esa Tanner and Seelina Rogers were both married by a License on the 15th of Feb., 1774. (in English)

Johannes Floerl and Dorothea Kiefer were both united in Christian marriage Feb. 22, 1774. The wedding text: Psalms 31:20-24.

Mr. Christoph Kraemer and Catharina Hengleiter were both united in Christian marriage March 1, 1774. Text: Ephesians 5:21-31.

Johann Friederich Lackner and Johanna Margaretha Schubtrein were both united in Christian marriage March 8, 1774. Proverbs 8:33-36.

David Harris and Sarah Bevel were both married together by a License on the 11th of March, 1774.

Samuel Royall and Verlinder Godbee of St. Georg's Parish were both lawfully married on the 27th Day of March, 1774. (in English)

John Holzendorff and Elisabeth Ehrhardt were both married by a License on the 1st Day of April, 1774. (in English)

Samuel Pace and Mary Glasher, both of this Parish, were lawfully married on the 18th of Dec., 1774. (in English)

Robert Bevil and Sarah Hudson, both of this Parish, were married by a License on the 27th of Dec., 1774. (in English)

1775

Salomo Zant and Dorothea Rieser were both united in marriage by Sen. Muhlenberg, Jan. 31, 1775. Text: Psalms 73:25-26.

Benjamin Glaner and Hannah Margaretha Bach were both united in marriage Feb. 7, 1775.

John Dannell and Hannah Dammans were both lawfully married on the 26th of Feb., 1775. (in English)

Johann Georg Maurer and Maria Sybille Saecht were both united in Christian marriage March 27.

John Little and Mary Shewman, both of Carolina, were both lawfully married on the seventh Day of Nov., 1775. (in English)

1776

William Samson, Capt. of a vessel, and Mary Anne Kirk were both married on the 4th Day of April, 1776 after they had subscribed a Bond of indemnification at any time and in all events. (in English)

1777

John Merkel of Goshen and Susanna Hover were both united in marriage by a license from the Governor in Goshen, May 13, 1777.

Jacob Strohbard and Judith Jourdine, both of Carolina, were married by a License from Governor Burrow in Carolina on the 29th Day of April, 1777. (in English)

Johannes Maurer and Anna Mueller, widow of Joh. Paul Mueller, were both united in marriage July 1, 1777. Text: Psalms 143:8, 9, 10. "Lord, teach me to do Thy will."

John Venieur and Elisabeth Winkler, both of Purrysborough, were married lawfully in the Month of Aug., 1777.

Johann Georg Winkler, a widower, and the widow Maria Rieser, were both united in marriage Sept. 30.

1778

Mr. Johann Adam Treutlen, late Governor of this State, and Mrs. Anna Unselt, widow, were both united in marriage the 14th of Jan., 1778. Text: Hebrews 13:8. "Jesus Christ the same yesterday and today."

John Bilbow, Capt. of a Company of Horses, and Jane Hudson of this State Spinster, have been married on giving Security the 12th of Feb., 1778. (in English)

Jacob Ihle and Jane Border, a widow, both of Effingham County, have been joined by a License on the 10 Day of March, 1778. (in English)

Christian Jonathan Zipperer and Gratiosa Zittrauer have been married by a License on the 10th Day of March, 1778. Text: I Timothy 4. (in English)

Joh. Christopher Buntz and Hannah Elizabeth Hangleiter have been married on the 13 of March, 1778. Text: I Thessalonians 3:12, 13. (in English)

William Kennedy and Elisabeth Treutlen, both of this State, have been married on the 8th Day of April, 1778. Text: Luke 15, v. 11. (in English)

The Revd. Mr. Joseph Cook and Anne Boullin, both of Carolina, have been married on the [left unfilled] of May, 1778. (in English)

Matthaeus Biddenbach and Apelonia Kiefer were both united in Christian marriage July 28, 1778. Text: Ephesians 5:25-33.

Christopher Baile and [left unfilled] Welsh, both of the State ? of ? Georgia ? have been married the 18th Day of May, 1778. (in English)

Abraham Fred. Jackocho and Jenny Kain have been married the 25th of Aug., 1778. (in English)

Daniel Weitman and Miss Salome Lemke were both united in Christian marriage Oct. 28, 1777. Text: Isaiah 61:10. "I will greatly rejoice."

William Kennedy and Elizabeth Quillen were married the 1778.

Jerusalem Church Records
Burials

1755

Regina Hueber, a child of about 10 years, died in Bethany on her father's plantation of a consumptive disease.

Johannes Leimberger, a child of 5 years, died peacefully April 30, 1755.

Mary Hueber, a child of 9 years, died on the 6th of March, and was buried the next day.

[A baptismal entry follows here, evidently by mistake, and is stricken out.]

Joh. Ulrich Fezer's little son was born May 31, and received the baptism of necessity immediately after birth and then died right afterwards.

Ursula Oexle, a child of almost 3 years, died June 4, 1755, and received Christian burial here the next day.

Jacob Leimberger died in the evening of June 29, 1755, and was buried July 1.

Sarah Steiner, a girl who went to Holy Communion in the Preparation, died Oct. 4, 1755, on Charles Flerl's plantation at the age of 15 years and 2 months, and on the next day she was buried out there.

Peter Schubdrein died in Bethany, Oct. 8, 1775, and received Christian burial the next day.

Israel Christian Heid died Nov. 27, 1775, and was buried the next day.

1756

Johann Christoph Bunz died Jan. 17, 1756, and was buried on the 18th, the 2 Sunday after Epiphany.

Barbara Heinle died March 22, 1756, of a consumptive disease at the age of 47 years.

Christian Mackh, a child of 6 week, died March 25, 1756, and received Christian burial the same day.

Georg Rahn, a child of 3 years and something over a month old, died March 26, 1756, and was buried the next day, the 27th.

Johann Martin Rahn, a child of 8 days, died April 16, 1756, and was buried on the 18th, the first day of Easter.

Margareth Franck died April 22, 1756, of epilepsy. She was almost 10 months old.

Johann Caspar Weber died April 15, 1756. He lived only 8 days.

Jacob Hueber died June 25, 1756, in Bethany, of a consumptive disease at the age of 54 years, and was buried the next day.

Henriette, the little daughter of Mr. Johann Christoph Bornemann and his wife Caroline Magdalene, died on a journey from Halifax to Ebenezer, and was buried there Sept. 25, 1756.

William McDanell also died about this time.

Peter Kohleisen died in Ebenezer Oct. 6, 1756, of a protracted disease, and was buried on the 7th.

Louisa Margaretha Greves died Oct. 10, 1756, of a consumptive disease in Ebenezer, and received Christian burial on the 11th with a funeral sermon.

Johann Michael Fezer, a child of 14 months, died on the night between Oct. 18 and 19 and was buried on the 19th, 1756.

Susanna, daughter of James Waston of Mount Pleasant, died at Ebenezer, Oct. 20, 1756 at the age of 9 months.

Elizabeth Waston of Mount Pleasant, age 19 years, died Oct. 27th in Ebenezer, and was buried the next day.

Friederica Maria Schubdrein, age 1 year and 10 1/2 months, died Oct. 29th, 1756, and was buried the next day.

Friederich Fincke, a child of almost two years, died Nov. 5, 1756, and received Christian burial on the 6th.

Hannah Elisabeth Schneider, a child of 3 years, died Nov. 7, 1756, and was buried on the 8th.

Johannes Honold died Nov. 22, 1756, and was buried on the 23rd in the plantation cemetery.

Johann Bernhard Geiger, a child of about 6 1/2 years, died Nov. 30, 1756, and was buried the next day in the cemetery of Zion Church.

Georg Eigel died Dec. 7, 1756, of a fever at the age of 56 years, and was buried on the 8th in Zion Church cemetery.

Up to this point the deceased were reported to England on Dec. 16, 1756.

1757

Adam Straube died in the night between Jan. 2 and 3, 1757, and was buried the next day.

Christoph Kronenberger, a child of 1 year and 9 months, died Jan. 23, 1757, and was buried the next day.

Maria Magdalena Mohr died July 28, 1757, at the age of 1 year and 10 months, and received Christian burial on the 29th in Bethany.

Michael Walliser died in the night of July 31 and Aug. 1, and was buried Aug. 1, 1757. He had dropsy and was in his best years when he died.

John Conrad Gnann died Aug. 18, 1757 in Bethany, and was buried the 19th, at the age of 1 1/2 years.

Johann Georg Schneider's wife gave birth to a stillborn child Aug. 20, 1757.

Johann Georg Fischer, a child of 1 year and 6 months died at Bethany, Aug. 22, 1757, and was buried the next day.

Hans Michael Schneider died after a brief illness Sept. 27, 1757, at the age of 66 years. He was buried the next morning in Zion Church cemetery.

N. B. — Shortly afterwards his daughter-in-law, the wife of J. G. Schneider, died.

Maria Elisabeth Lechner died Oct. 18, 1757, of epilepsy at the age of 2 months.

Johann Peter Schubdrein, a child about 1 1/2 years old, died Oct. 16, 1757, and was buried the following Monday the 17th.

Hanna Elisabeth Ziegler, a child of 8 months, died Oct. 21, 1757, and was buried on the 22nd.

Lucas Geiger, the upright schoolmaster on the plantations, died in the night before Oct. 31, 1757, and was buried on the 31st.

Andreas Fischer, a child, died Nov. 6, 1757, at Bethany and was quietly buried on the same day.

Johann Georg Bunz, a child of 1 1/2 years, died Nov. 13, 1757.

Anna Catharina Graeve, née Heinrich, died Nov. 21, 1757, and was buried on the 22nd.

Johann Jacob Tussing, a child of 3 months, died Nov. 25, 1757, and was buried the next day.

Anna Catharina Paulitsch, a child, died Dec. 1, 1757, on the Savannah River, and was buried on the 3rd.

Jacob Israel Buerck, a child of 2 months, died Dec. 17, 1757, and was buried on the 18th.

Maria Schubdrein, daughter of Joseph Schubdrein, died Dec. 23, 1757, at the age of 14 months and was buried the next day.

Maria Elisabeth Niess died Dec. 22, 1757, and the next day received Christian burial at the age of 1 year and 7 months.

Anna Ursula Heck died in the night of Dec. 23 and 24, 1757, and was quietly buried.

Anna Maria Friederica Thilo died Dec. 24, 1757, and was buried the next day.

1758

Salomo, a son of the deceased Johann Peter Schubdrein, died Jan. 6, 1758, and received Christian burial at Bethany.

Paul Zittrauer died Feb. 1, 1758 of a breast ailment, and was buried on the 2nd. He was 44 years old.

Anna Maria Lackner, a child of 4 years, died Feb. 1, 1758, and was buried on Feb. 2 following.

Israel Maurer died in the night of Feb. 1, and was buried Feb. 1, at the age of 8 days.

Maria Magdalena Weber died March 3, 1758 in Goshen at the age of 4 weeks.

Anna Catherina Fischer, a native of Langenau, died after a protracted sickness in Bethany, March 15, 1758, and received Christian burial there the next day. Her age was 30 years and 1 month.

Michael Oechsle died March 23, 1758, and was buried on the 24th. His age was about 16 years.

Johann Adam Biddenbach, son of Matthaeus Biddenbach, died April 9, 1758, and was buried the next day. He was 2 1/2 years old.

Martin Lackner, the elder, died on his plantation at Habercorn, April 13, 1758, and was buried the next day on his plantation.

Christian Gerber died May 1 in the evening, and received Christian burial on the 2nd. He was 8 years old.

Agatha Burgsteiner died May 8, 1758, and on the 9th received Christian burial in the Zion Church cemetery.

Johann Paulus died May 20, 1758 in Bethany, and was buried on the 21st in Jerusalem Church cemetery. His age was 16 years.

Maria Hapacher died at the age of 20 years on May 24, 1758, and was buried on the 25th.

Anna Catharina Moser died of a protracted sickness on June 1, 1758, and was buried on the 2nd. Her age was 47 years.

Catharina Remshardt died June 10, 1758, of a protracted disease at the age of 43 years, 5 months and one day.

Johann Melchior Oechsle died June 11, 1758, and was buried on the 12th at the age of 12 years.

Friedrich Gottlieb Schweiger died June 14, 1758, and was buried the same day.

Valentin Deppe died June 24, 1758 from the fatal bite of a rattlesnake, and was quietly buried on the 25th.

Christian Fetzer, a boy of 17 years, died July 8, 1758 at Kornberger's, and was buried on the 9th.

Sibylla Gschwandel died Aug. 5, 1758, and was buried on the 6th. She was 60 years of age less about 3 months.

Jonathan Treutlen died Aug. 29, 1758, and was buried the next day. His age 8 days.

Hanna Remshardt died in the night of Oct. 27, 1758, at the age of 10 months.

Ursula Eigel, aged 58 years, of Duerrenberg in the Archbishopric of Salzburg, died Nov. 8, 1758, and was buried on the 10th.

1759

Johann Michael Hirsch died in the night between Jan. 24 and 25, 1759, and was buried on the 26th. He was 50 years and 7 months old.

Friedericka Margareth Bollinger died March 10, 1759, and was buried on the 12th. She was 2 years and 9 months old.

Anna Rau died April 10, 1759. She was 62 years old.

Christian Buntz died May 4, 1759, and was buried the same day at the age of 4 days.

Anna Gerber, 9 years and 11 months old, died May 13, and was buried on the 14th, 1759, in Bethany.

Christian Oechsle, a child of two years, died May 16, 1759, and received Christian burial in Bethany.

Hanna Elisabeth Arnsdorf died May 16, 1759, and was buried on the 17th.

Daniel Deppe died June 3, 1759, and was buried on the 4th.

Catharina Margaretha Eischberger died July 24, 1759, and was buried on the 25th at the age of 12 years and 4 months.

Johannes Deininger died July 28, 1759, and was buried on the 29th, at the age of 14 days.

Maria Barbara Michel, a child almost 2 months old, died Oct. 7, 1759, and received Christian burial on the 8th.

Caroline Catharine Weitmann died Oct. 16, 1759, and was buried on the 17th.

Jonathan Maurer died Oct. 24, 1759, and was buried on the 25th, at the age of 18 days.

Maria Maurer, wife of Gabriel Maurer, died Nov. 25, 1759, and was buried the next day.

Christian Israel Wertsch, a child of 10 days, died early on Dec. 2, 1759, and was buried on the same day.

Georg Kiefer died Dec. 3, 1759, and was buried on the 4th, at the age of about 33 years.

Christiana Elisabeth Treudlin died Dec. 9, 1759, and was buried on the 10th. Her age was 2 years and 9 months.

N. B. — Up to this point those deceased have been reported.

1760

David Zettler died in the night of Jan. 26, 1760, and was buried on the 27th, at the age of 5 years and 5 months.

Elisabeth Schneider, née Sanftleben, about 62 years old, died March 13, and was buried on the 14th, 1760.

John Gottlieb Lackner died March 13, in the evening, and was buried on the next day. He was 10 years, 6 months and 3 weeks old, less one day.

Anna Margaretha Schweiger died April 9, 1760, and was buried on the 10th at the age of 5 years and 8 weeks.

Christian Riedelsberger, aged 45 years, died March 30, 1760, and was buried the next day in the plantation cemetery.

William Alexander, a man of something more than 30 years, died April 23, 1760, and was buried on the 24th in the town cemetery.

Daniel Birck, 2 months old, died April 24, 1760, and was buried in the evening of the same day.

Anna Rosina Hammer, 43 years old, died May 6, 1760, and was buried on the 7th in the town cemetery.

Maria Reinlaender died in Savannah in the night of May 15, 1760, which was Ascension Day, and was buried there on the 16th. She was 21 years and 5 months old.

Elisabeth, the daughter of Martin Taescher, 7 1/4 years old, died May 22, and was buried the next day.

Jacob, the middle son of Gabriel Maurer, died June 6, 1760, and was buried the next day. He was 7 years and 9 months old.

Maria, a baptized Negro girl, died on Capt. Kiefer's plantation June 10, 1760, and was buried on the 10th in the town cemetery. She was 3 1/2 years old.

Wilhelmina Ernestina Michler, a child of 8 years and 8 months, died in the evening of June 18, and was buried on the 19th in Bethany.

Josua Taescher died June 25, 1760, and was buried the 26th in the town cemetery. His age was 2 1/2 years less 5 days.

Dorothea Lackner, a child of 3 1/2 years, died June 26, 1760, and was buried on the 27th in the town cemetery.

Christian Fetzer died June 26, 1760, and was buried the next day in the plantation cemetery near Zion Church. His age was 2 years and 6 weeks.

Jonathan Ihle died June 29, 1760, and was buried on the 30th in the plantation cemetery near Zion Church. His age was 9 months.

Esther Zettler, a child of 15 months and 17 days, died July 9, 1760, and was buried July 10.

Johannes Michler died July 17, 1760, and was buried on the 18th. His age was 7 years and 5 months less 3 days.

Maria, the wife of Joh. Georg Niess, died July 19, 1760, and was buried on the 20th, which was the 7th Sunday after Trinity. Her age was 28 years.

Samuel Schmidt, 18 years old, died July 20, and was buried the next day.

Gottlieb, the youngest son of John Rentz, died in the night between Oct. 5 and 6, and was buried on the 6th.

Elisabet Graeves died Oct. 30, 1760 before day, and was buried in the afternoon. Age 1 year, 1 1/2 months.

Johann Christoph Fetzer died in the night between Oct. 29 and 30, 1760, and was buried in the afternoon of the 30th. Age 2 months and 8 days.

N. B. — Up to this point the deceased have been reported to the Society.

Eva Regina Schweiger, 47 years old, died Dec. 26, 1760, and was buried on the 27th in the plantation cemetery.

1761

Georg Gross, 45 years old, died in Bethany Feb. 3, 1761, and was buried there on the 4th.

Thomas Geschwandel, 66 years old, died on his plantation March 8, 1761, and was buried on the plantation cemetery on the 10th.

Judith, a daughter of Balthaser Kiefer, somewhat over three years old, died early on April 8, and was buried the next day on his plantation.

Matthias Seckinger died July 22, 1761 before day and was buried in the afternoon of the same day in the town cemetery. He was 44 years old.

Michael Mackh, a child of 17 months, died in Bethany, Nov. 4, 1761, and was buried there on the 5th.

Friederica Margaretha Bollinger, 2 years and 2 months old, died early on Nov. 12, 1761, and was buried in the afternoon in Bethany.

Matthaeus Groll, 12 years old, was born in Niederstotzingen, and died in Ebenezer, Nov. 17, 1761, and was buried the next day in the town cemetery.

Catharina, a Negro girl, who was born and baptized on June 27, 1753, died on the Minister's Plantation Nov. 19, 1761, and the next day received Christian burial.

Hanna Elisabet, youngest daughter of Dan. Schubtrein, 1 1/4 years old, died in the evening of Nov. 22, and was buried on the 23rd.

David Neidlinger, a child of 11 months, died Dec. 4, 1761, and was buried on the 5th.

Samuel Schubtrein, 2 years and 8 months old, died Dec. 13, 1761, and was buried in the plantation cemetery on the 14th.

N. B. — Up to this point the deceased have been reported.

1762

Maria Magdalena Graeves died May 5, 1762, and was buried on the 6th in the town cemetery. Her age was 5 years and [left unfilled].

Johann Andreas Heintz, a child of 8 months, died May 21, 1762, and was buried on the 22nd in the plantation cemetery.

Christian Israel Graeves, 8 years and 11 months old, died in the evening of June 14, 1762, and was buried on the 15th towards evening.

Johannes Haid, a child of 4 years and 4 months, less 4 days, died June 19, 1762, and was buried on the 20th.

Benaja Wertsch, a child of 7 months less 4 days, died June 25, 1762, and was buried on the 26th.

Johannes Heinle, 1 year and 6 months old less 3 days, died June 27, 1762, and was buried on the 26th.

Leonhard Krause died June 29, 1762, and was buried on the 30th in the plantation cemetery.

Rebecca Niess, 3 years and 8 1/2 months old, died early before day June 30, 1762, and was buried towards evening of the same day.

Elizabet Gnann, a child of 4 years, died July 5, 1762, and was buried on the 6th.

Clara Straub died Aug. 10, 1762, and was buried on the 11th in the plantation cemetery.

Lorentz Eigel died Oct. 3, 1762, and was buried on the 4th.

Joh. Adam Klein died Oct. 4, 1762, and was buried on the 5th. His age was 3 years.

Amalia, a baptized Negro girl, died Aug. 14, 1762 in the night and received Christian burial on the 15th in the town cemetery. Her age 1 year and 1 month.

Lydia Waldhauer, a child of 2 years, died Aug. 16, and was buried on the 17th in the town cemetery.

[left unfilled] Unseld died Nov. 9, 1762, and was buried on the plantation cemetery on the 10th. His age, 70 years.

Ruprecht Eischperger died Nov. 13, 1762, and was buried on the 14th.

Angelica Heckel died Nov. 24, 1762, and was buried on the 25th in the town cemetery. Her age [left unfilled].

Up to this point the deceased have been reported.

1763

Christian Thomas Eischperger died March 17, 1763, and was buried on the 18th. His age 19 years.

Maria Dorothea Haefner, the oldest daughter of the deceased Mrs. Straub, died on Hauesler's plantation April 17, 1763, and was buried there. She was about 30 years old.

Ursula Fetzer, 44 years old, died July 17, 1763, and was buried on the 18th.

Christian Leimberger died early on July 22, 1763, in the 54th year of his age, and was buried on the same day.

Catharina Paulus, a child of 13 years, died July 23, 1763, in the evening and was buried on the 24th.

Catharina Wertsch died Aug. 16, 1763, and was buried the next day.

Elisabeth Hammer died Aug. 24, 1763, and was buried on the 25th. Her age 20 years.

Anna Dorothea Fischer, about 42 years old, died in Bethany Oct. 3, 1763, and was buried on the 4th.

Salome Schweickhofer, a child of 9 months, died Oct. 4, 1763, and was buried on the 5th.

Gideon Kiefer, a child of one year and 9 months, died Oct. 8, 1763, and was buried on the 9th.

Samuel Schubtrein died Oct. 10, and was buried in the evening of the same day. His age 1 year, 8 months, 2 weeks and 4 days.

David, the son of Gabriel Maurer, 7 years and 8 months old, died on Wednesday evening, Nov. 2, and was buried the next day on the plantation cemetery.

Daniel Rieser, a child of 4 years and 7 months, died in the night before Dec. 6, 1763, and was buried in the cemetery at Bethany on the 7th.

N. B. — Up to this point the deceased have been reported to the Society.

1764

Bartholomeus Mackh died Jan. 12, 1764, and was buried on the 13th in Bethany. His age was 34 years and 2 months.

Christian Gravenstein, a child of 9 days, died in the night before Feb. 13, 1764, and was buried on that day in Bethany.

Regina Heintz died Feb. 10, 1764, of pain in the side and was buried Feb. 11. Her age, 38 years.

Timothaeus Birck, a child of 6 months, less 6 days, died early on March 11, and was buried towards evening.

Ludwig Eigel died March 17, 1764, and was buried on the same day.

Maria Catharina Pechtle died early on April 26, and was buried towards evening of the same day. Her age was 4 years and 10 months. 1764.

Barbara Fetzer, 44 years old, died May 1, 1764, and was buried the next day.

Carl Flerl died May 2, 1764, and was buried the next day. His age [left unfilled].

Lucia Metzscher, a child of 2 years, died May 21, 1764, and was buried on the 22nd.

Tobias Fischer, a child of 2 years and 4 months, died July 8, 1764, and was buried on the 9th in Bethany.

Margaretha Schubtrein was 79 years old, died July 21, 1764, and was buried the next day in the town cemetery.

Anna Margareta, the 8-year-old daughter of Finck, died in Bethany Aug. 24, 1764, and was buried the next day in the town cemetery.

Maria, the youngest daughter of Christian Steiner, 5 months old, died Sept. 18, 1764, and was buried the next day in Zion's cemetery.

Catharina, the daughter of Balth. Rieser, 6 months old, died in Bethany in the night between Sept. 24 and 25, and was buried the next day.

Johannes Riedelsperger, 11 years old, died in Ebenezer Oct. 1, 1764, and was buried the next day.

Israel, the son of Joh. Pflueger, died Oct. 9, 1764, and was buried the next day.

Gabriel Nathaniel Riedelsperger died in the night between Oct. 3 and 4, and was buried on the 4th. His age 13 3/4 years.

Catharina Dorothea Leitner died in Bethany Nov. 2, 1764 in the evening, and was buried on the 4th in the town.

Sebastian Hasenlauer of Langenau died Nov. 21, 1764, in the evening, and was buried on the 23rd in the town cemetery.

Peter Hammer, a 13-year-old inhabitant of Ebenezer, died in the night before Dec. 4, 1764, and was buried on the 5th.

N. B. — Up to this point the deceased have been reported to the Society.

Georg Waldhauer, a child of one year, died Feb. 18, 1766, and was buried on the 19th.

Christian Leberecht Rieser, a boy of 11 years, died April 23, 1766, and was buried on the 24th in Bethany.

Gabriel Maurer died March 1, 1766, and was buried on the 2nd in the plantation cemetery.

1765

Benaja Schweikhofer died Aug. 11, 1765, and was buried on the 12th.

1766

Maria Buntz, a child of 2 years, died June 2, 1766, and was buried on the 3rd.

Margaretha Schweikhofer died in the night before June 5, 1766, and was buried on the same day in the town cemetery. She attained an age of over 83 years.

Maria Magdalena Schubtrein, a child of 9 months, died July 7, 1766, and was buried on the 8th here in the town cemetery.

Hans Maurer died early on Aug. 31, 1766, and was buried towards evening.

Hanna Margareta Leimberger died Sept. 3, 1766, and was buried on the 4th. Age 13 months.

Michael Scherer, a stranger among us, died Sept. 15, 1766, and was buried on the 16th.

Abdi, a baptized Negro child belonging to Joh. Gruber, died Sept. 11, 1766, and was buried on the 12th with the usual Christian ceremonies. Age, 2 years, 8 months.

Obadja Pechtle, a child of 7 months, died Sept. 12, 1766, in the evening, and was buried on the 13th.

Angelica Oechsle died Oct. 30, early in the night, and was buried on the 31 in Bethany, 1766.

Samuel Graves died in the night of Oct. 30, 1766, and was buried in the evening of the same day.

Mrs. Gertraut Boltzius, widow, entered into eternal rest by a blessed death early on Nov. 7, 1766, and was interred on the 8th in the town cemetery. She was in the 48th year of her age.

Judith Flerl, a child of 9 months, died Oct. 10, 1766, and was buried on the 11th in Zion cemetery.

Martin Lackner died Nov. 12, 1766, and was buried on the 13th in the town cemetery. He was about 56 years old.

Apollonia Gress died in Bethany in the evening of Nov. 22, 1766, and was buried on the 23rd in the town cemetery.

Salome Schubtrein, a child of something more than 3 months, died Nov. 23, 1766, and was buried on the 24th in Zion cemetery.

Salome Schneider, a child of 3 months, died early on Nov. 24, 1766, and was buried the same day in Zion cemetery.

Georg Kogler died early on Nov. 27, 1766, and was buried in the evening of the same day.

Maria Heinle died Nov. 30, 1766, and was buried the next day. Her age, 28 years less 25 days.

Joh. Caspar Waldhauer died early on Dec. 3, 1766, and was quietly buried in the evening of the same day. Age, 70 years.

Joh. Theobald Kieffer, an important member of Ebenezer congregation and a faithful deacon of the same, entered into his rest Dec. 7, 1766, and received Christian burial on the 8th with the attendance of many members of the congregation.

Christian Hesler died in the night before Dec. 21, 1766, and was buried on the 22nd.

N. B. — The deceased have been reported up to this point.

1767

Anna Catharina Bidenbach, a child of 3 years and 10 months, died Jan. 11, 1767, and was buried on the 12th in Bethany.

Joseph Leitner died Jan. 4, 1767, in the night, and was buried the same day.

[left unfilled] Roth, wife of the surgeon Roth, died Jan. 20, 1767, and was buried on the 21st in the town cemetery.

Josias Rieser died early on the 21st, and was buried toward evening of the same day. His age was 14 years, less 15 days. He was buried at the same time as Mrs. Roth.

Johannes Meyer died Jan. 23, 1767, and was buried on the 24th in Bethany.

Barbara Bollinger died in the night before Jan. 29, 1767, and was buried in the afternoon of the same day.

Hans Schmidt, a man of 60 and some years, died Feb. 8, 1767, and was buried on the 8th. The funeral text was Revelations 14:13: "Blessed are," etc.

Johannes Scheraus died March 23, 1767, and was buried on the 24th. Funeral text: Mark 13:37. His age [left unfilled].

Michael Weber died in Bethany May 17, 1767, and was buried on the 18th in the town cemetery.

Elisabeth Hesler died Sept. 20, 1767, and was buried on the 21st. Her age, 57 years.

Appollonia Mueller died Sept. 23, 1767, in the evening, and was buried on the 24th.

Georg Ludwig Roth died Oct. 27, 1767, and was buried on the 28th. He was a Catholic.

Daniel Remshardt died Oct. 29, 1767, and was buried on the 30th in Zion cemetery.

Johannes Schuehle died Nov. 23, 1767, and was buried on the 24th. His age, 15 years.

Johann Georg Schneider died Nov. 30, 1767, and was buried the next day in the plantation cemetery.

Johann Christoph Roth, a child of one year, died early on Dec. 8, 1767, and was buried in the afternoon.

1768

Beata Hangleiter died Jan. 24, 1768, and was buried on the 25th.

Hanna Friederica Kornberger died Feb. 9, 1768, and was buried on the 10th in Zion cemetery.

Samuel Rieser, a child of 5 days, died Feb. 10, 1768, and was buried on the 11th.

Veit Landfelder died Feb. 13, 1768, and was buried on the 14th, which was Esto mihi Sunday, in the town cemetery.

Daniel Schubtrein died Feb. 15, 1768 early at 2 o'clock in the night and was buried the next afternoon.

Friedrich Freyermuth, a child of 17 days, died early on Feb. 11, and was buried toward evening of the same day.

Daniel Schubtrein, a child of 2 months and 3 weeks, died March 9, 1768 in the evening, and was buried on the 10th.

Mr. Herman Heinrich Lemcke, until now the second minister of the Lutheran congregation at Ebenezer, died on April 4, 1768, on the second Easter day in the morning at a quarter past 4 o'clock. On the following day his body was accompanied to the town cemetery by many sorrowing relatives and parishioners and laid to rest by the ministers' burial marker. He was in the 48th year of his life and in the 23rd of his office. The funeral text was taken from Isaiah 45:15.

Ursula Landfelder died May 31, 1768, and was buried June 1, Her age, 51 years, less 3 months.

Anna Bexle, a girl about 10 years old, whom Michael Weinkauf had adopted, died June 4, 1768, and was quietly buried in the cemetery at Bethany.

Elisabet Catharine Zettler, as I firmly believe, entered into the rest of the people of God on June 9, 1768, and received Christian burial on the 10th.

Anna Maria Pflueger, a child of 9 years, died Aug. 4, 1768, and was quietly buried on the 5th.

Israel Schubtrein, a child about 15 hours old, died Aug. 24, 1768, and was quietly buried.

Christina Ochs, a child about 3 years and 10 months old, died Aug. 30, 1768, and was quietly buried on the 31st at Bethany.

Hanna Maurer, a child almost 8 years old, died Oct. 23, 1768, and was buried the next day.

Georg, a Negro boy, who belonged to the estate of the deceased Mr. Lemcke, died Oct. 29, 1768.

Anna Maria Eischberger died in the night between Oct. 30 and 31, 1768, and received Christian burial on Nov. 1, 1768, in the 58th year of her age.

Georg Faul died in the night before Nov. 5, 1768 in the 44th year of his life, and received Christian burial on the 6th. God had granted him repentance unto life.

Maria Brandner, a widow, aged 65 years, died Dec. 11, 1768, in the night, and on the same day received Christian burial.

Up to this point the number has been reported.

1769

Anna Maria Fetzer died Jan. 14, 1769, and was buried the next day. Her age was 52 years.

Eleonora Heid died of a breast ailment on Jan. 20, 1769, in the evening and was buried on the 22nd at the age of 39 years.

Matthaeus Zettler died Feb. 3, 1769, and was buried the next day.

Jacob Rudolph Staeheli, a young man about 23 years old less 3 months, died Feb. 6, 1769, and was buried the next day.

Ursula Buerck died in the night between March 12 and 13, 1769, and was buried on the 14th in the 34th year of her age.

Hanna Schweighofer died April 1, 1769, and was buried on the 2nd at the age of 29 years and 9 months.

Obadjah Rahn, a ten-year-old boy, died April 28, 1769, and was buried on the 29th.

Maria Oexle, a child of 8 days, died April 28, 1769, and was buried on the 29th.

Christina Weinkauf died May 1, 1769, and was buried on the 2nd at the age of 25 years.

Waldpurga Bollinger died March 3, 1769, and was buried on the 4th.

Michael Maurer, a child of almost 4 years, died May 25, 1769, and was buried on the 26th.

Mrs. Hanna Elisabeth Wertsch died June 17, 1769, and on the 18th received Christian burial. With infirmity of body for many years she attained the age of 31 years, less two months.

[left unfilled], a stranger, died June 18 at Mr. Wertsch's place, and was quietly buried the same day.

Friedrich Epinger was found dead in Old Ebenezer Creek on June 18, 1769, judicially disposed of on the 19th, and for the time buried at said creek.

Maria Magdalena Bechtel, 12 years old, died July 14, 1769, and received Christian burial on the 15th. Text: Psalms 119:94.

Angelica, née Heinle, died June 11, 1769, and received Christian burial on the 12th.

Johann Christoph Rheinlaender died July 10, 1769, died near Goshen and was buried on the 11th at Goshen at the age of 2 years.

[left unfilled] Scraggs, wife of Drury Scraggs, an English woman, died Aug. 1, 1769, and was buried on the 2nd in the cemetery here. Her age was 30 years.

Johann Martin Reilaender, 5 years old, died Aug. 28, 1769, on Strohbarth's plantation in Goshen, and was buried Aug. 29 on Zipperer's plantation. Text: Psalms 84:2.

Regina Ochs, 9 years old, died Aug. 26, 1769, and was buried Aug. 27 at Bethany.

Ursula Kiefer died early on Sept. 2, 1769, in the 69 year of her age, and was buried the same day. Text: Hebrews 12:23.

Georg Schleich died Aug. 27, 1769, and received Christian burial on the 28th with a funeral sermon on John 8:24 in the cemetery at Zion Church. His age was some 30 years.

Friedrich Ochs in Bethany died Sept. 12, 1769, and received Christian burial on the same day in the cemetery at Bethany. The funeral sermon was on I Timothy 1:15. His age was 69 years.

Johann Kraus, a child of 15 months, died Sept. 15, 1769, and was interred on the 16th in the cemetery at Zion Church.

Eliezer, Johann Hangleiter's Negro boy, died in the third year of his age Sept. 25, 1769, and was buried towards evening with a sermon.

Johann Ulrich Fezer, several months old, died and was buried Oct. 7, 1769. Text: Psalms 84:11.

Heinrich Ludwig Gravenstein died Oct. 28, 1769, and received Christian burial on the 30th in the cemetery at Bethany. His age, 4 years and 7 months.

Christiana Candace, Christoph Friedrich Triebner's Negro child, 4 days old, died Oct. 29, after receiving baptism, and was buried in the evening.

Christian Friedrich Scheel, from Weyerbach in Germany, died Nov. 8, 1769, and was buried Nov. 9, here in Ebenezer.

Maria Rahn died Nov. 14, 1769, and was buried on the same day in the cemetery here.

Matthaeus Fischer, 2 years and 3 months old, died Dec. 3, 1769, and was buried on the 4th at Bethany.

Ludwig Weidmann, 43 years old, died Dec. 20, 1769, and received Christian burial the next day in the cemetery here. Psalms 110:3.

Samuel Heinle, 3 weeks old, died Dec. 30, 1769, and was buried the next day in the cemetery at Zion Church.

Up to this point the number has been reported.

1770

Christian Geiger died Jan. 25, 1770 in the 14 year of his age, and was buried Jan. 26 in the cemetery at Zion.

Gideon Kosch, a Negro child, died Feb. 19, 1770, and was buried in the afternoon of the same day in the cemetery here.

Georg Fischer, 5 years old, died Feb. 20, 1770, and was buried on the 21st in the cemetery at Bethany.

Magdalene Reiter died April 4, 1770, in the 52 year of her age, and was buried inn the cemetery at Zion Church.

Johanna, the child of Ulrich Neidlinger, 3 weeks old, died May 14, 1770, and was buried the next day in the cemetery in Ebenezer.

Christian Bittenbach died May 5, 1770, in the 60 year of his life, and received Christian burial the next day in the cemetery at Bethany. The funeral text was Matthew 6:19-21.

Anna Fezer, 2 years old, died May 23, 1770, and was buried on Ascension Day.

Christiana, the daughter of Nicolaus Schubdrein, died May 29, 1770, in the 6th month of her life, and was buried the next day at Zion.

Sebastian Fezer, an aged man, died July 4, 1770, and was buried in the cemetery at Zion.

Georg Rens died July 27, 1770, and was buried July 28 in the cemetery at Ebenezer.

Johann Friedrich Ernest, surgeon, a native of Breusland, died Aug. 5, 1770, being the 8 Sunday after Trinity, and was buried on the afternoon of the same day in the cemetery at Ebenezer.

Salome Zant, a child of 2 years, died Aug. 30, 1770, and was buried the same day in the cemetery just named.

Hanna Rentz, the widow of the Rentz just noted above, died Aug. 20, 1770, and was buried on the 21st.

Anna Margaretha Biddenbach was taken in mercy out of this vale of tears into heaven Aug. 31, 1770, and received Christian burial at Bethany Sept. 1.

Elisabeth Heinle, a child 9 months old, died in the night before Sept. 24, 1770, and was buried on the 24th.

Christoph Aug. Gottlob Triebner, a child of 8 days, died Aug. 16, 1770, and on the next day was buried here in the cemetery in the ministers' burial place. A babe is more before God's throne than a grown spoiled son.

Johann Peter Arnsdorff, a year old, died Oct. 13, 1770, and was buried the next day here in the cemetery.

Johannes Floerl, 60 years old, died Oct. 19, 1770, and received Christian burial on the following Sunday with a funeral sermon here in the cemetery.

Maria Catharina Meyer died Oct. 23, 1770, and received Christian burial on the next day. Her age is 50 years and one month. Funeral text: Job 19, v.

Georg Heid died Oct. 28, 1770, and was buried the next day.

Maria Dorothea Greiner died Nov. 4, and was buried the next day.

Sophia Frank died Nov. 5, and was buried the next day.

Johannes Kornberger died Nov. 12, 1770, and was buried the next day.

Johann Georg Deininger, 58 years old, died Nov. 14 in the evening, and was buried on the 15th.

Sophia Frank, 14 years old, died Nov. 6, 1770, and received Christian burial the next day at Bethany. [Cf fifth entry above.]

Maria, infant daughter of Johann Deininger, died Nov. 23, 1770, and was buried the next day.

Barbara Habor, wife of Michael Habor, died Nov. 22, 1770, and was buried on the same day. Her age was 70 years.

1771

Phoebe, a baptized Negro child belonging to Mrs. Lemking, died Feb. 18, 1771, and was buried the next day.

Johann Michael Bohrman died Feb. 17, 1771, and was buried on the 19th here at Ebenezer.

Matthias Schubdrein, 5 months old, died [left unfilled], 1771, and was buried in Zion Church.

Anna Eva, daughter of Johannes Scheeraus, died at the age of 3 years and 2 months, and was buried June 3, 1771, here at Ebenezer.

Andreas Greiner of Halifax died June 19, 1771, and received Christian burial on the 20th in the plantation cemetery.

Anna Maria Kemler died July 11, 1771, and was buried July 12 in the cemetery at Ebenezer. Her age was 17 years. Funeral text: I Peter 1:24, 25.

Johan Georg Eppinger, 3 1/2 years old, died Aug., 1771, and was buried the next day at Bethany.

Asa Remshardt, 10 months old, died Aug. 21, 1771, and was buried at Zion.

Maria Steiner, 4 years old, died Aug. 25, 1771, and was buried the next day at Zion.

N. Harret, English, 16 years old, resident with her brother, Mr. Harret on Weinkauf's plantation, died Aug. 26, and was buried Aug. 28, at Bethany.

David Eischperger, 60 years old, an old Salzburger, died Aug. 29, 1771, in the mill, and was buried the next day at Zion.

Maria Margaretha, daughter of Johan Georg Zittrauer, 2 years and 9 months old, died Aug. 31, 1771, and was buried the next day.

Maria, daughter of Georg Ziegler, 8 years old, died Sept. 7, 1771, and was buried the next day.

Jacob Mohr, 60 years old, died Sept. 7, 1771, and was buried the next day at Ebenezer.

William Ewen Waldhauer, 2 1/2 years old, died Sept. 11, 1771, and was buried the next day.

Salomo Kiefer, 3 years and 2 months old, died Sept. 28, 1771 in the night, and was buried the next day.

Samuel Heinle, one year old, died Sept. 18, 1771, and was buried the next day.

Georg Glaner, a Salzburger, 63 years old, entered into his rest Oct. 8, 1771, and was buried the next day. Funeral text: Revelations 5:5: "Weep not, behold the Lion," etc.

David Unselt died after being bedridden for 14 days from a fall from a horse at a hateful race Oct. 24, 1771, and was buried the next day.

Catharina Maria Rens, 1 year and 10 months old, died Nov. 3, 1771, and was buried the next day.

Johannes Oechsle, 13 years old, died Nov. 16, 1771, and was buried the next day at Bethany.

Friedrich Lackner died Dec. 10, 1771, from a blow from an axe, which crushed his skull and robbed him of his senses, received 14 days before at work on the royal road. He was buried Dec. 11, 1771, in the cemetery at Zion.

Up to this point the number reported.

1772

Caspar Waldhauer's daughter died Jan. 20, 1772, immediately after receiving lay baptism.

Johann Adam Freyermuth died as a child of 2 years and 2 months, Feb. 5, 1772, and was buried in the cemetery here.

Salome, daughter of Samuel Kraus, 6 years, 1 month and 3 days old, died Feb. 5, 1772, and was buried the next day at Zion.

Johann Paul Mueller, Jun. died Feb. 21, 1772, in the 27th year of his age, and was buried on the 22nd. Text: Psalms 55:19: "He hath delivered my soul in peace."

Anna Maria Schubtrein died in the night before March 17, 1772, and was buried the same day.

Salome Remshardt, a child of a week, died March 18, 1772, and was buried the next day.

Georg Heckel died April 6, 1772, and was buried the next day. Text: Luke 10:20, 21.

Georg Niess died April 10, 1772, and was buried the next day. Text: Job 19:25 "I know."

Krause's stillborn child was buried June 27, 1772 in the cemetery at Zion.

Jacob Lange, 25 years old, died Sept. 20, 1772, and was buried in the cemetery at Zion.

Christian Friedrich Hekel, 3 days old, died Oct. 7, 1772, and was buried the next day.

Christina, wife of Johannes Heinle, died 3 hours after the birth of a daughter early at 3 o'clock on Oct. 8, 1772, and was buried the same day.

Benaja, Salomon Zant's son, 3 years old, died Nov. 11, 1772, and was buried the next day.

Up to this point the number reported.

Thomas Schweighofer died Dec. 7, 1772, and was buried the next day on his plantation.

Barbara Koegler, 60 years old, died at 11 o'clock in the night of Dec. 31, and was buried on New Year's Day in the cemetery at Zion.

1773

Elisabeth Zant, 26 years old, died Jan. 1, 1773, and was buried the next day in the cemetery at Ebenezer. Funeral text: Hosea 13:14.

Hanna Marg. Remshardt and Christina, her newborn child, both died Jan. 31, 1773, and were buried the next day in Zion.

Maria, wife of Joseph Schubtrein, died Feb. 6, 1773, and was buried the next day at Zion.

William Makai, a child of 3 months, died Jan. 29, 1773, and was buried on the 30th.

Johannes Heinle's stepson, son of Johann Georg Schneider, died in the month of March, 1773, and was buried the next day, but no notice was given here.

David Steiner's newborn child died April 3, and was buried the following Sunday at Zion.

Hanna, daughter of Joh. Scheeraus, 10 years old, died April 14, and was buried the next day.

Johann Ulrich Fezer died suddenly April 19, and was buried the next day at Ebenezer.

Anna Barbara, daughter of Joh. Friedrich Epinger, died May 28, 1773, and was buried the same day at Bethany.

Hanna Norssler died Aug. 16, 1773, and was buried the next day here in the town.

Hanna Margaretha Kraemer died Sept. 6, 1773, and was buried the next day.

Margaretha Niess, a widow 66 years old, died Oct. 10, 1773, early, and was buried the same day.

Jacob Gnann, 44 years old, died Oct. 13, 1773, and was buried the next day.

Christian Steiner's little son died Oct. 11, 1773, and was buried the next day at Zion.

Jacob Gnan in Bethany died Oct. 14, 1773, and was buried the same day. Funeral text: Psalms 90.

Rahel Mohr died Oct. 28 as one who, 15 years ago, was excommunicated on account of adultery which she confessed to me, and was buried Oct. 29 without the presence of the minister, although there was preaching to the parishioners present.

Johannes Floerl, a child of 4 years, died Nov. 15, 1773, and was buried the next day.

Johanna Hangleiter, 4 years old, died Nov. 23, 1773, and was buried the same day.

Johanna Friederika Niess, 4 years old, died Nov. 25, 1773, and was buried the next day.

Ursula Hangleiter, 44 years old, died Dec. 6, 1773, and was buried the same day. Funeral text: I Peter (?) 1:17, 18.

Hanna Floerl, 90 years old, died Dec. 12, 1773, and was buried the next day.

So far.

1774

Anna Mary Floerl, 61 years old, died Jan. 18, 1774, and was buried the next day. Funeral text: Luke 12:32 and 11:42.

Daniel Reihlaender, 4 years and 3 months, died Feb. 2, 1774, and was buried on the third.

Mr. Urban Bunz died Nov. 18, 1774, and was buried the next day with a funeral sermon in Jerusalem Church. Funeral text: 2 Timothy 1:10, "Christ hath abolished death."

1775

Conrad Haus, a man born in Pennsylvania, died Jan. 1, 1775, and was buried the same day.

1776

Nicolaus Cronenberger died in the 59th year of his age Jan. 8, 1776, and was buried on the 9th in Ebenezer cemetery.

Michael Rieser died Feb. 21, 1775, and was buried Feb. 22. Funeral text: Psalms 55:19. "The Lord hath delivered me in peace."

Margaretha Huber died in the night between March 31 and April 1, and was buried April 1.

Johann Paul Miller died April 11, 1775, and received Christian burial the next day.

Johann Georg Maurer died April 16, 1775, and was buried on the second Easter day.

Maria Magdalena Maurer died Oct. 11, 1775, and was buried the next day.

Johanna Friederika Reinlaender died Oct. 15, 1775, and was buried the next day.

Wolfgang Mack died in the month of Nov., 1775, and was buried the next day at Bethany.

Johann Martin Reilaender died in the 40th year of his age Jan. 16, 1776, and was buried the next day. Funeral text: Galatians 3:13, 14.

Maria Magdalena Maurer, a woman in childbed, died Oct. 11, 1775, and was buried the next day.

Hanna Margaretha Maurer, a widow, died Nov. 30, 1775, and was buried the next day.

Timotheus Lemke died in the best bloom of his age in his 24 year, Feb. 9, 1776, and was buried the next day. Funeral text: Isaiah 45:15. "Verily thou art a God that hidest thyself."

Mrs. Catharina Lemke, widow of the former pastor, Rev. Herman Heinrich Lemke, entered into her rest by a blessed death Feb. 21, 1776, and was buried in the cemetery at Ebenezer after she had attained an age of 59 years and 3 months. Funeral text: Psalms 55:19. "The Lord hath delivered me in peace."

Nathanial Biddenbach, 13 years old, died July 13, 1776, and was buried the same day in the cemetery at Ebenezer.

1777

The widow Reinier died Jan. 2, 1777, and received Christian burial the next day.

Johannes Klein, a husband of about 40 years, died March 29, 1777, and was buried the next day.

The widow Glaner died after an illness of 8 days April 7, 1777, and received Christian burial the next day.

Tobias Freyermuth, a child of 4 years, died April 30, and was buried the next day.

David Pflueger, 11 years old, died Sept. 10, 1777, and received Christian burial the next day.

Anna Margaretha, daughter of Matthias Biddenbach, 13 years old, died Sept. 17, 1777, and received Christian burial the next day.

Johannes Pflueger, 16 years old, died Sept. [left unfilled], 1777, and received Christian burial the next day.

Barbara Pflueger died Nov. 16, 1777, and received Christian burial on the 17th.

Johann Christoph Kraemer died Nov. 14, 1777, and received Christian burial the next day.

Johannes Hekel died Nov. 30, 1777, and received Christian burial Dec.1.

Salomo, son of Johannes Maurer, 2 years old, died Dec. 24, 1777, and was buried the next day.

1778

Salome Zant died in her 32d year March 10, 1778, and was buried the next day. Psalms 25:17.

Miss Catharina Bolzius died in the 36th year of her age March 9, 1778, and was buried on the same day. Funeral text: 2 Peter 3:15.

Christina Rieser died April 14, 1775 in the 8th year of her age, and received Christian burial on Palm Sunday.

Johann Georg Bunz, a boy of 17 years, died June 7, 1778, on the same second day of Pentecost on which he, with other children, should have gone for the first time to communion. The funeral text stands Sirach 2:21, 22, 23.

Anna Biddenbach died in the 37th year of her age April 27, 1778, and received Christian burial the next day.

Hanna Elisabeth Sekinger died July 14, 1778, and received Christian burial the next day.

Conrad Deininger, 18 years, died Nov. 8, 1778, and received Christian burial the next day.

1779

Hanna Elizabeth Bunz died in the 20th year of her age in childbed Feb. 3, 1779. Psalms 135:8.

Johann Casper Werthsch died June 24, 1779, and received Christian burial the next day.

Mrs. Anna Barbara Rabenhorst died July 1, 1779, and was buried the same day at Zion.

Hanna, the 6 months old daughter of Joh. Rudolph Binninger, died Aug. 19, 1779, and was buried the next day.

Catharina Gravenstein died Aug. 27, 1779, and was buried the same day.

1780

Ulrich Neidlinger died Nov. 21, 1780, and was buried on the 28th. Funeral text: Matthew 25. "Those prepared entered in to the wedding with him."

Joseph Schubtrein died Nov. 30, 1780, and was buried the same day. Funeral text: Isaiah 22. "All flesh is as grass and all its goodliness."

David Steiner died Dec. 1, 1780, and was buried on the 2nd. Funeral text: Matthew 25.

Salomo Schrempf died Nov. 1, 1780, and was buried on Nov. 2. Matthew 25. "And the door was closed."

1781

Anna Ursula Paulus died peacefully in the Lord, Jan. 28, 1781, and was buried the next day. Funeral text, 2 Timothy 3: "I have fought a good fight."

Anna Margaretha [left unfilled] died Feb. 12, 1781, and was buried the next day at Zion. Funeral text: 2 Corinthians 5: "God was in Christ, etc."

Christian Zipperer in Goshen died Feb. 15, 1781, and was buried on the 18th. Funeral text: Hebrews 9:23: "It is appointed unto men once to die." Hebrews 4:1, 2, 3.

Jacob Mezger died Feb. 16, 1781, and was buried on the 17th.

Christina Kieffer died in the 23rd year of her age, Dec. 14, 1781, and was buried the next day.

Maria Elisabeth Freyermuth died in the 33rd year of her age, March 31, 1781, and was buried April 2.

Nathanael Kieffer died Jan. 8, 1800.

GENEALOGICAL INDEX
(by GFJ)

Explanation

The index to the previous edition of these church records is a name index, not a person index. That means that it lists all names, without indicating whether they represent one person or more than one. For example, there are entries for Barbara, Maria, and Barbara Maria Heinle, with no clue that they are all the same person. The casual reader may be surprised to read that Friedericke Margaretha Bollinger died on March 10, 1759, but was born on August 21, 1759. This can, of course, be explained by the custom of giving the name of a deceased child to the next child of the same sex born to the family, as we also see in the cases of Gravensteins, Helmles, Kraemers, and other families. Fortunately, the fact that a single name refers to two children can usually be confirmed by recourse to the birth and death lists, but sometimes the pertinent entries are missing; and it often occurs that an infant's death is recorded whereas its birth was not. Similar confusion exists in the case of married women when the entry merely says "so-and-so and his wife." Sometimes the name of the wife is revealed elsewhere, but sometimes it is not. Also, on a later occasion, the "and his wife" may refer to another woman, she being a second or third wife, as can often be proved by the marriage register.

In addition to all the above snares, which are common to church records in all languages, the German records are made even more difficult by a peculiar system of name-giving. Nearly all the Christian names in these records combine those of two saints and are therefore of Hebrew, Greek, or Latin origin. The only old Germanic names are those of popular rulers such as Carl, Franz,

Friedrich, Heinrich, Ludwig, Otto, Ruprecht, Siegmund, and Wilhelm; and even the Franzes, Ludwigs, Ruprechts, and Carls of Ebenezer may have owed their names to St. Francis, St. Louis, St. Ruprecht (patron saint of Salzburg), and Charlemagne (popularly thought to have been a saint).

The first Christian name was almost invariably that of a saint, most often Johann, Maria, or Anna, and it was not uncommon for several sons and daughters of a family to have Johann, Maria, or Anna as a first name. That was feasible because the second name was the *Rufname*, or the name by which one was called in social life and often in the German records. For example, Johann Martin Boltzius and Johann Adam Treutlen were always called Martin and Adam, never Johann. The English records, on the other hand, list Boltzius and Treutlen by their first names.

The practice of listing by either first or second or both names makes the records confusing since Johann Jacob Metzger can be listed as Jacob Metzger, Johann Metzger, or Johann Jacob Metzger. This index has tried, as far as possible and using outside sources, to list all persons under their complete names. For example, if Theobald Kiefer and Johann Kiefer are married to the same woman at the same time, then both entries must refer to Johann Theobald Kiefer. On the other hand, Johanna Lackner could be identical with either Johanna Christina Lackner or Johanna Margaretha Lackner, but we can not determine which. Since Johannes Kronberger appears but a single time, he is most likely the same as Johannes Jacob Kronberger, who appears eleven times, but we have no proof of this.

If the reader cannot immediately find a Georg or a Magdalene, he should also search under Johann Georg or Maria Magdalena or under any other combination of names. Individuals bearing the same name are distinguished by Roman numerals. I and II may distinguish father from son or mother from daughter, or perhaps the deceased and the still living child with the same name, but they sometimes differentiate between unrelated people sharing the same name. When known, the maiden names of married women are given, as well as that of their future husband(s) if they remarry (indicated by *see*).

The local residences of families are sometimes given, these being mainly Bethany, Mount Pleasant, Briar Creek, New Goettingen, Halifax, and Beaver Dam, all up the Savannah River from Ebenezer; and Purysburg downstream on the South Carolina side and Abercorn on the Georgia side, with Josephs Town and Goshen slightly to the south of them. Of more interest to genealogists are the homes in the Old Country, including Gastein, Loigam, Mietosil, Rastadt, and Werffen in Salzburg; Duerrenberg, a principality next to Salzburg; Durlach, a principality on the upper Rhine; Albeck, Altheim, Bermeringen, Bernstadt, Gaerstetten, Holtzkirch, Langenaltheim, Langenau, Langensee, Nerenstetten, Niederstozingen, and Leipheim in the Territory of Ulm; Weiher (Weyer in Alsace); and the unlocated places Weyerbach and Breusland.

In addition to these mostly South German places, there are also the cities of Frankfurt on the Main, Chemnitz in Saxony, Goettingen in Brunswick (Braunschweig), and the homes of the North German pastors: Forst in Lusatia, Kroppenstedt in Sachsen-Anhalt, Fischbeck in Schaumburg, Pagenkoep in Pommerania, and Poesneck in Thuringia.

When a family name appears in varied spellings, the variants are listed and cross-referenced to the standard form. The genealogies of many of the families listed here are given in the *Georgia Salzburger and Allied Families*, ed. Pearl Rahn Gnann and revised by her daughter Amy Gnann LeBey (Southern Historical Press, PO Box 1267, Greenville, SC 29602).

In writing my *Salzburger Saga* (Athens, Ga., 1984), I used great care in indicating family relationships, but a gentleman in California wrote to assure me that Pastor Boltzius would never have condoned his ancestors siring children by two women at the same time. It turned out that there were two unrelated men of the same name producing families in Ebenezer. If the reader discovers any such discrepancies, I will appreciate hearing of them for the benefit of future genealogical research.

George Fenwick Jones   University of Maryland

Genealogical Index

Brunson (Graves County)
  Anna, d J 8
  Johann 8
  Mary, w J 8
Bucher
  Catharine, w JC 95
  John Cothal 95
Buehler
  Christiana Elisabeth, née
    Bechtol, w J I 63, 75,
    77, 82, 101
  Jacob I 63, 64, 75, 77, 82,
    101
  Jacob II, s J I 63
  Johanna Juliana, d J I 75
  Juliana Christiana, d J 82
  Maria, adopted d J I 77
  Maria Elisabeth 92, see
    Freyermuth
Buehner
  Maria, w M 54
  Michael 54
Buerck, see Birck
Buerkstein
  Maria 66
Buntz, Bunz (fr Bethany)
  Anna Barbara, d U 22
  Anna Barbara, w JG I 1, 14, 24,
    33, 41, 50, 69, 70, 80
  Anna Margaretha, w U 8, 22,
    41, 58, 60, 62, 64, 69, 70
  Anna Maria, d JG I 50, 121
  Barbara, w HL 22, 36, 41, 42,
    60, 62
  Christian, s JG I 14, 111
  Christiana, d JG I 41
  Hannah Elizabeth, née
    Hangleiter, 2nd w JC I 104,
    140

Heinrich Ludwig, s U 14, 16,
  36, 41, 42, 60, 62
Johann Christoph I, s U 1, 8,
  69, 77, 80, 104, 106
Johann Christoph II, s JCh I
  77
Johann Georg I 1, 14, 20, 24,
  33, 41, 43, 50
Johann Georg II, s JG I 1, 109
Johann Georg III, s JG I 24,
  139
Johann Heinrich 55
Maria, d JG I 33, 121
Mr. & Mrs. 32
Urban 8, 22, 41, 52, 58, 60,
  64, 69, 70, 137
w Johann Christoph 77
Burcksteiner
  Daniel 52, 54, 57, 58
  Maria, née Daescher, w D 54,
    58, 95
  Salome, d D 58
Burgermeister (fr Purysburg)
  David, s HCh 73
  Heinrich Christoph 73
  Johann Martin 92
  Margaretha, w HCh 73
Burgsteiner
  Agatha 110
  Daniel 47, 60, 95
  Maria, w D 60, 95
  Maria Elisabeth 92, see
    Mengersdorf
Burnell
  John 100
  Winefred, née Wilson, w J 100
Burrow
  Governor 103
Burrysburry, see Purysburg

Dorothea, d JM 66
Elisabeth, d JM 113
Elisabeth, w JM 2, 7, 9, 11, 58,
    66
Johann Martin 2, 7, 9, 11, 17,
    18, 26, 32, 49, 57, 58, 60, 66,
    79, 113
Josua, s JM 7, 32, 114
Maria 95
Salome, d JM 79
Ursula, w JM 2, 7, 9, 11, 17, 18,
    20, 26, 32, 43, 49, 57-61, 66
Daley
    Benjamin 65, 66, 101
    Elisabeth, d B 65
    Susannah, née Garneth, w B 65,
        101
Dammans
    Hannah 102, see Dannell
Daniel
    Elisabeth, née Dison, w J 99
    Josiah 99
Dannell, Danell
    Elisabeth 100
    Hannah, née Dammans, w J 102
    John 102
Dasher, see Daescher
Dauner, (fr Langensee)
    Apollonia d M 91, see
        Leimberger
    Michael 86
    Waldpurga, wid Oechsele, w M
        86
Davey
    Mary 99, see Matthew
Davis (fr Mount Pleasant)
    David, s N 74
    Elizabeth, d N 74
    Jane, wid Southerland, w T 88
    John 1, 2

Mary, w J 2
Mary, w N 74
Nathan 74
Sarah, d J 2
Thomas 88
de Trushit
    Charles 69
Deal
    Charles 63
    Lydia, d C 63
    Mary, d C 63
    w Charles 63
Deininger
    Anna Barbara, w JG 15, 18,
        21, 27
    Catharina, d JG 27
    Conrad, s JG 21, 140
    Johann Georg 15, 18, 21, 27,
        41, 131
    Johannes, s JG 15, 112
    Maria, d JG 41, 131
Depew
    Alley 100, see Hall
Depp, Deppe (fr Purysburg)
    Daniel, s V 9, 112
    Johanna 101, see Preisier
    Maria Margaretha, w V 1, 9,
        88, see Gnann
    Valentin 1, 9, 111
Descher, see Daescher
Dickson, Dixon
    Josias 45
    Judit 95
    Robert 97
    Sarah 97, see Schrempf
    Suky, née Johns, w R 97
    Thomas, s J 45
    w Josias 45
Dieter
    Rebeka 79

Groll (fr Niederstotzingen)
Anna Catharine 47, 95, see
Freiermuth
Anna Margareth 68
Maria Ursula 84, see
Paulus
Matthaeus 115
Gronau
Friedrika Maria 46, 95, see
Triebner
Hanna Elisabeth 87, see
Wertsch
Gross
Georg 115
Groves
Allen 95
Mary, w A 95
Gruber
David, s GI 56
Elisabeth I, née
Schwartzwaelder, w G I 19,
28, 43, 46, 56, 88
Elisabeth II, d G I 43
Georg I 19, 28, 46, 56, 77, 88
Georg II, s G I 19, 46
Johann I 40, 47, 58, 81, 92
Johann II, w J I 40
Johann Jacob, s G I 28
Josua, s J I 58
Maria Magdalena, née Kalcher,
w J I 40, 47, 76, 81, 92
Salome, d G I 77
Salomo, s G I 47
Wilhelm, s J I 81
Grumbling, Grumbley
Elizabeth I, née Fulsher, w
V 70, 100
Elizabeth II, d V 70
John, s V 70
Valendine 70, 100

Gschwandel
Sibylla 111
Thomas 115
Gugel
Anna Maria, née Schubdrein,
w J I 4, 11, 17, 22, 28, 32,
45, 53
Daniel, d M 41, 42
David, s J I 32
Hannah Elisabeth 99, see
Michel
Johann Christoph, s J I 4
Johannes I 4, 11, 22, 28, 32,
40, 45
Johannes II, s J I 22
Josua, s J I 45
Matthias 42
Salome, d J I 28
Samuel, s J I 11
w Matthias 42
Habercorn, see Abercorn
Haberer
Anna Eva, wid Weidmann, w
JM 57, 63, 98
Johann Michael 57, 63, 98
Habor
Anna Eva 80
Barbara, w M 131
Michael 131
Haeck, Heeck, Heck
Angelica, d C 24
Anna, d C 13
Anna, w C 4, 13, 18, 20, 24,
43
Anna, d G 13
Anna Ursula 109
Caspar 4, 13, 18, 24, 43
Georg 13
Johannes, s C 43
Margaretha, d C 4

Margaretha née Gunther, w R 3,
   5, 43
Maria, d R 4, 5, 24, 88, see
   Rheinlaender
Maria Magdalena d A 18, 92,
   see Gruber
Ruprecht 13
Keller
   Johann Adam 24
Kemler
   Anna Maria 132
Kennedy, Canady
   Elisabeth, née Treutlen, w W
      104
   Hugh 5, 17, 86
   Ottilie, wid Schrempf, w H 4, 5
   William I 104
   William II, s H 5
Kessler
   Adam 97
   Hanna, née Kieffer, w A 97
Kettle, Kettel, Kittel (fr
   Carolina)
   Elisabeth I, née Dannel, w
      Pet 69, 100
   Elizabeth II, née Kiefer, w Jac
      61
   Jacob, s Pet 61, 69
   John, s Jac 61, 69, 73
   John Reignier, s Pet 69
   Mary Neuman, w John
   Nancy, d Joh 73
   Peter, s Jac 69, 100
   Polly, w Joh 73
Kiebler, see Kuebler
Kiefer, Kieffer (fr Purysburg)
   Anne Maria, née Winnagler, 2nd
      w F 86
   Apelonia 104, see Biddenbach
   Balthaser 115

Christian 66
Christina 60, 70, 77, 81, 141
Dorothea I, née Reuter, w JJ
   45, 55, 59, 75, 93
Dorothea II, 2nd w JJ 75, 102
Elisabeth 38, 93, see Zant
Emmanuel, s JT 14
Georg, s JT 5, 112
Gideon 118
Hanna, d G 5, 39, 53, 97, see
   Kessler
Hanna Elisabeth, née Depp, d
   JJ 55
Hanna Margareth, w I 65
Israel, s JT 5, 65, 79
Jacob Friedrich 5, 86
Joel, s JJ 59
Johann Jacob 45, 55, 59, 75,
   93
Johann Theobald 3, 5, 11, 14,
   23, 34, 123
Josua, s I 65
Judith, d B 115
Lydia, d JJ 75
Maria I, w F 5
Maria II, née Bacher, wid
   Meyer, w JT 5, 11, 14, 34
Mr. & Mrs. 23, 26, 27, 30, 33
Mr. 29, 33, 38, 39
Mrs. 33, 36
Nathanael 141
Salomo, s JJ 45, 132
Ursula 128
w Friedrich 5
w Georg 5
King
   James, s W I 76
   Sarah, née Goldwire, w W
      I 68, 96

William I 68, 76, 96
William II, s W I 68
Kirk
  Gideon 71
  Mary Anne 103, see Samson
Kittle, see Kettle
Klein
  David, s J 25, 52
  Hanna Elisabeth, d J 40
  Johann Adam, s J 16, 117
  Johannes 16, 25, 31, 40, 52, 85,
    138
  Jonathan, s J 31
  Maria Christina, née Oechsele, w
    J 16, 25, 31, 40, 52, 85
Klock (fr Purysburg)
  Barbara, née Schaeffer, w C 85
  Caspar 85
Knoll
  Anna Margaretha 62
Kogler, Koegler (fr Rastadt)
  Barbara, wid Riedeberger, wid
    Schaefer, w G 4, 5, 7, 16,
    21, 135
  Elisabeth, d G 18, 24, 29, 33, 39,
    48, 96 see Wertsch
  Georg 7, 16, 122
  Johannes, s G 16
  Maria, d G 89, see Heinle
Kohleis, Kohleisen
  Angelica 14
  Peter 106
Kornberger, see Kronberger
Kraemer, Kramer
  Anna Catharina, née Hangleiter,
    w JC I 65, 68, 72-75, 77, 79,
    82, 102

  Hanna Margaretha née
    Mueller, 2nd w JC I 4, 5,
    8, 9, 11, 20, 21, 22, 24, 28,
    32, 34, 37, 42, 44, 45, 47,
    53, 57, 136
  Johann Christoph I 1, 4, 5, 8,
    9, 11, 18, 19, 22, 23, 25,
    32, 34, 37, 42, 43, 45, 47,
    53, 57, 62, 65, 66, 68, 72-
    75, 77, 79, 82, 102, 139
  Johann Christoph II, s JCh I
    65
  Johann Christoph III, s JCh I
    83
  Salome, d JC I 72
Kraeuter
  Walpurg 93, see Oechsele
Kraus, Krauss, Krause
  Barbara, née Einecker, w L
    10, 13, 19
  Elisabeth, d S 55
  Jacob 79
  Johann 128
  Judith, née Flerl, w S 32, 38,
    39, 41, 43, 44, 46-48, 51,
    53, 54, 55, 57, 58, 66,
    71-73, 75, 81, 91
  Leonhard 10, 13, 14, 16, 19,
    116
  Margaretha, d Jac 79
  Mr. & Mrs. 24
  Mr. 16, 26
  Mrs. 14, 23
  Salome, d S 39, 133
  Samuel 32, 38, 39, 41, 43, 46,
    47, 51, 53-55, 57, 58, 60,
    65, 66, 71-73, 75, 81, 91,
    133
  Susanna, w Jac 79

Jacob 134
Maria Magdalena, w Dr. 78
Lanier
　Bansamon 64
　Eolef, w B 64
　John, s B 64
　Mary 95
Larrimor
　James 19
　John, s J 19
　Mary, d J 19
　Rebecca, w J 19
　Sarah, d J 19
Lastinger (fr Langenaltheim)
　Andreas, s J 76
　Anna Barbara, née Huber, w
　　J 44, 62, 69, 81, 93
　Elisabeth, d J 76
　Hanna, d J 44
　Johann Georg, s J 69
　Johannes 44, 62, 69, 76, 81,
　　93
　Maria, d J 81
Lechner, see Lackner
　Dorothea, d V 12
　Maria, w V 3, 5, 11, 12
　Maria Elisabeth, d V 5, 108
　Veit 3, 5, 11, 12
Leen
　Elisabeth Catharina, née Zettler,
　　w L 92
　Lambeth 92
Leimberger (fr Loigam in
　Salzburg)
　Apelonia, née Dauner, w ChI
　　37, 51, 65, 71, 81, 91
　Catharina, d ChI 71
　Christian 118
　Christian Israel, s Chr 37,
　　44, 51, 65, 71, 76, 81, 91

David Postumus, s ChI 81
Hanna Margareta, d ChrI
　37, 121
Jacob 105
Johannes I, s ChI 105
Johannes II, s ChI 71
Margareth 16, 22, 91, see
　Jansen
Salome, d ChI 51
Samuel, s ChI 65
Leitner (Leiter)
　Catharina Dorothea 120
　Joseph 16, 25, 31, 123
Lemcke, Lemke (fr Fischbeck)
　Catharina, née Kroehr, wid
　　Gronau, w HH 1, 5, 6,
　　10, 13, 18, 20, 21, 23, 25,
　　26, 30, 34, 36, 37, 38, 41,
　　43, 51, 56, 138
　Herman Heinrich 3, 6, 13, 14,
　　20, 24, 25, 26, C, 31, 36,
　　37, 40, 41, 43, 56, 125, 138
　Johanna Christiana, d HH 40,
　　47, 51, 52, 54-57, 63, 64,
　　76, 77, 82
　Salome, d HH 63, 68, 71, 104,
　　see Weitmann
　Timotheus, s HH 47, 56, 63,
　　64, 68, 71, 138
Little
　John 103
　Mary, née Shewman, w J 103
Lloyd
　Thomas 46
Lohrmann (fr Ulm)
　Jacob, s J 78
　Johann 70, 78, 89
　Susanna, née Humbart, w J
　　78, 89

Margaretha, d JL 14
Maria, d H 2
Maria, d JL 31
Maria Catharina 131
Maria Fanciska, w H 2, 17, 30,
    52
Mr. & Mrs. 18, 28, 31
Mrs. 20, 36
Salome, d H 17
Sarah, d H 30
    w Jacob 15, 24
Michel
    Hannah Elisabeth, née Gugel, w
        N 99
    Johann 6, 16, 32, 34, 36, 48, 56,
        58, 66, 72, 81
    Maria Barbara, d J 16, 112
    Maria, w J 14, 16, 34, 48, 53,
        56, 58, 66, 72, 81
    Nikolaus 99
Michler (fr Nerensteten)
    Catharina 75
    Johann 43, 44, 51, 56, 114
    Maria, w J 1, 24, 33, 44, 51, 56,
        61
    Wilhelmina Ernestina 114
Mick, Mickh
    Jonas 3, 11
    w Jonas 3, 11
Milbrook
    William 71
Miles
    Ann, d A 59
    Aquila 59
    Henriette, w Aquila 59
Millen
    Gottlieb, s S 12
    Stephan 12

Miller (see Mueller)
    Abigail, d D 68
    Daniel 68
    James 67
    Jane, d J 67
    Nathaniel 81
    Rose, d J 67
    Sarah, d N 81
    Sarah, w D 68
    Sarah, w N 81
Milliner
    Mary, née Goodall, w W 101
    William 101
Mohr (fr Goshen)
    Anna Maria w Jac II 88
    Elisabeth, wid Walliser, w J I
        20, 30, 49, 87
    Jacob I 19, 87, 132
    Jacob II, s J I 20, 30, 34, 43,
        132
    Johanna 92, see Fetzer
    Maria Magdalena 108
    Rahel 136
Mollet
    Bartholomeus, s D 42
    Daniel 42
    Mary, w D 42
Moon
    Diana 98, see Radliff
Moor
    Sarah 81
Moore
    Elisabeth 96, see Goldwire
    Nancy 81
    Susannah 78
More
    Aaron 45
    Grace, w A 45
    Mary 94
    Sarah, d A 45

Morisson
    Adam 83
    Elisabeth, w A 83
    Sarah, d A 83
Moser
    Anna Catharina, wid Kuebler, w
        L 88
    Anna Ursula 90, see Fettler
    Lucas 88
Moses
    Jacob 6
    w Jacob 6
Mott
    Abraham 95
    Sarah, w A 95
Mount Pleasant 3, 5, 11, 87, 107
Muehberg, Muehlenberg, (fr
        Pennsylvania)
    Heinrich Melchior 65
Muehler
    Johann 51
    Maria 4, 51
Muek (Mueck)
    Catharina, w JC 81, 82
    John Caspar 81, 82
    Matthias 82
    w Matthias 82
Mueller
    Anna, née Seckinger, w JP II 53,
        96, 103, see Maurer
    Anna Margaretha 91, see
        Remshardt
    Anna Maria, d G 7
    Appollonia, née Maurer, 2nd w
        JP I 124
    Elisabeth, née Maurer, w JP I
        24, 36, 37, 50, 58, 86, 94
    Friedrich Wilhelm, s JP I 4, 29,
        50
    Georg 7

Johann Georg 85
    Johann Paul I 36, 37, 50, 58,
        94, 137
    Johann Paul II, s JP I 58, 96,
        103, 133
    Rosina, wid Schubdrein, w JG
        7, 13, 85, 121
Muets
    John Caspar 72
Murray
    John 67
Nail
    David Conrad, s JC 67
    John Conrad 67
    Rose, w JC 67
Negro
    Aaron, Zettler's boy 22
    Abdi, Schweighofer's boy 31
    Adam, Kieffer's boy 38
    Amilia, Lemke's girl 26, 117
    Anna, Triebner's girl 50
    Brandner's boy 37
    Carl, von Muench's boy 24
    Catharina, Hangleiter's girl
        83
    Catharina, Kiefer's girl 33
    Catharina, Rabenhorst's girl
        29, 116
    Christian, Mills' boy 21
    Christian, Rabenhorst's boy
        39
    Christian, Schweiger's boy 31
    Christiana Candace, d David
        and Anna 50, 128
    Christine, Boltzius' girl 9
    Daniel, Lemke's boy 30
    Daniel, Rabenhorst's man 5
    David, Bunz's boy 69
    David, Rabenhorst's boy 31

www.ingramcontent.com/pod-product-compliance
Lightning Source LLC
Chambersburg PA
CBHW070426270326
41926CB00014B/2954